THE POTTERS' VIEW OF CANADA

Rare "Lake" pattern vase printed in green with Bartlett's Outlet of Lake Memphremagog. Ashworth. H. 25 cm.

ELIZABETH COLLARD

The Potters' View of Canada

Canadian Scenes on Nineteenth-Century Earthenware

McGill-Queen's University Press
Kingston and Montreal

© McGill-Queen's University Press 1983
ISBN 0-7735-0421-4
Legal deposit fourth quarter 1983
Bibliothèque nationale du Québec
PRINTED IN CANADA

Publication has been assisted by the Canada Council
under its block grant program.

Canadian Cataloguing in Publication Data

Collard, Elizabeth, 1917–
The potters' view of Canada
Includes illustrations of earthenware held by the
National Museum of Man, National Museums of Canada
Includes index.
ISBN 0-7735-0421-4
1. Pottery – 19th century – Great Britain – Themes,
motives – Canadian influences. 2. Pottery, English –
History – 19th century. 3. Pottery, Scottish –
History – 19th century. 4. Canada in art – History –
19th century. I. National Museum of Man (Canada).
II. Title.
NK4085.C64   738.3'09'034   c83-098603-0

For my husband

EDGAR ANDREW COLLARD

in gratitude for many things

and particularly for the joy of shared interests

(

CONTENTS

ACKNOWLEDGMENTS

For help with the preparation of this book I would thank in particular the Ontario Arts Council, which generously provided me with a grant to assist in carrying on the work, and the National Museum of Man, National Museums of Canada, whose staff aided me at every turn throughout the whole project. I owe special thanks to Frank Corcoran, assistant director, public programs, of the National Museum of Man, and Dr Frederick J. Thorpe, chief of the history division, for making essential material available to me. The planning for the book began in 1980, the idea having been born that spring during conversation with Barbara Riley, assistant chief (curatorial) of the history division. In the subsequent working out of the plan Judith Tomlin, curatorial assistant; Christine Grant, curator of collections; James Donnelly, registrar; and Jean Soublière, assistant registrar of the history division, gave me unfailing support. Harry Foster, the museum's photographer (national programs division), went to endless trouble on my behalf. It would be impossible to thank them all enough. I would only add that being associated with the history division, as the consultant on ceramics, has been one of my greatest pleasures during the last ten years.

Other museums were ready at all times to provide information. Dr Shirley Thomson, director of the McCord Museum, McGill University; Conrad Graham, the McCord's registrar; and Peter Winkworth, curator of prints and drawings, gave me combined help. Mary Allodi of the Royal Ontario Museum, Gary Hughes of the New Brunswick Museum, and Kathleen Campbell of the Winnipeg Art Gallery consulted their holdings on my behalf, as did Sharon Gater of the Wedgwood Museum, Barlaston, and John Munday of the National Maritime Museum, London, England. To Arnold Mountford, director of the City Museum and Art Gallery, Stoke-on-Trent, Staffordshire, I am deeply indebted, not only for much help with this book but for constant encouragement over the years in my task of documenting the historic link between Staffordshire and Canada's early ceramic trade.

Both the Public Record Office of Great Britain and the British Library provided assistance that was invaluable, and so did Josiah Wedgwood & Sons Ltd (through Alethea Wakefield of their Toronto office). The staff of the Public Archives of Canada, the National Library, and the National Gallery were consistently helpful. For aid with particular problems I would thank Susan Campbell, Michael Pantazzi, Brian Stewart, and Ann Thomas, all of the National Gallery of Canada. Erik J. Spicer, parliamentary librarian, Ottawa, made it possible for me to consult material not available elsewhere in Canada, and Daniel Pouliot, of the parliamentary library staff, spent much time in searching for it. William F.E. Morley, curator of special collections at the Douglas Library, Queen's University, endeavoured to find information which I needed.

Others who made it possible for me to obtain material which might otherwise have eluded me include Marnie R. Clarke, Wayne Curtis, Gerald Derick, Shirley Elliott, George Gibb, Ralph Greenhill, Ruth Jackson, Donald McLeish, A.J.H. Richardson, Ruth Robinson, John Russell, James Shakley, Norman Stretton, Christopher K. Swann, Barbara Gorley Teller, Rosslyn Tetley, and Helen Vechter. To the staff of McGill-Queen's University Press I am very grateful indeed, especially for the enthusiasm of David Norton, editor of the Press.

I owe most of all to my husband. For forty years he has, in his own historical writing, led others to sources which many would not have known of without his guidance. I am only one of a legion in debt to him.

THE POTTERS' VIEW OF CANADA

INTRODUCTION

This book deals with the views of Canada that appeared as decoration on nineteenth-century earthenware. During much of that century the name "Canada" belonged to certain parts of the country but not to others. Constitutional change and progress gradually brought the whole area together. It is in the modern inclusive sense that the word has been used. These are the potters' nineteenth-century views of what has become the Canada of today.

The type of wares dealt with are known as historical china in the United States. There the interest in collecting American scenes on pottery began well over a century ago. In Canada there was relatively little interest in Canadian views until a much later date. Today attitudes have changed and these wares are now among the most sought after by Canadian collectors. In every province museums are adding them to their holdings. The potters' views have become notable features of the widespread interest in Canadiana.

The appeal of these ceramic views is many-sided. They link the world of artists and printmakers and, as the nineteenth century advanced, the more "truthful" world of the photographer to the ceramics industry. They reflect taste in its changing moods, not only taste in the wares themselves (their bodies, shapes, colours) but a changing way of looking at things (from the romantic to the literal). As ceramic wares, these potters' views belong with the familiar objects of everyday use which are part of what has come to be called material history.

This is the first book to be devoted solely to potters' views of Canada, setting them against the historical background that explains the forms they took. The illustrations have been drawn from one of the most comprehensive collections of these wares in the country. Appropriately, it belongs to the National Museum of Man, Ottawa. This book is not, however, a catalogue, nor is it a "definitive" list. There will never be a definitive list. The unexpected is always possible and is always occurring. An example of the way the unexpected turns up is the view of Montreal seen on a tureen stand in Plate 17. This particular version of the scene, adapted from a published engraving of the 1830s, is a great rarity. It was completely unknown to collectors until it appeared not long ago at an auction sale of mixed goods in Scotland. The hope of finding a view hitherto unrecorded keeps collectors and ceramic historians on the alert.

The search is not only for the decorated earthenware itself but for the sources from which the potters derived their Canadian views. A number of these sources are known; others are still to be discovered. Some have come to light in surprising ways. The clearing out of an old writing box, whose contents had remained undisturbed for almost ninety years, disclosed a bundle of Christmas cards. Among the cards, received by a Montreal girl in 1882, was the first clue to the source used by a Scottish potter for his pictures of Canada. Eventually more of the cards whose sporting scenes were reproduced on table and toilet wares were brought to light. Some of them are illustrated here for the first time. A picture booklet salvaged by an antique dealer pointed to the source for another potter's views of Quebec. The Victorian photographer whose work was adapted for use on earthenware can now be identified. New information is also included on the dating of some of these wares.

All the wares considered are of an earthenware body, were decorated by means of transfer printing, and, with one exception, are nineteenth century in date. The exception, an eighteenth-century jug depicting the death of General James Wolfe on the Plains of Abraham (Plate 4), has been included because this scene on earthenware was the forerunner of the long series of nineteenth-century Canadian views and because nineteenth-century potters repeated it, with variations, on wares of their own.

The title of the book, *The Potters' View of Canada*, means that it is confined to wares with views taken within the boundaries of Canada or with Canadian symbols or personages. Some years after the War of 1812 British potters wooed customers in the United States with printed earthenware celebrating American victories. Canadians were certainly concerned with the outcome of battles in that war, but the events chosen for earthenware decoration were engagements fought outside Canada's boundaries. They do not fall within the potters' views of Canada.

The Canadian scenes commanded wide interest in their own day. Wares decorated with them had a sale in many parts of the world. They have been found in Canada itself, in the British Isles, and in the United States, and in places as far apart as Mexico and Portugal. The very fact that many of these wares were widely distributed when new, and were not made exclusively for the Canadian market, is historical evidence of the way Canadian scenery had seized the imagination and interest of the times. It places Canada (as it should be placed) not apart from the world but as part of it. In the nineteenth century, distance lent great enchantment to the view. Canada was regarded in various parts of the world as a romantic land where the old walled city of Quebec, the Gibraltar of the St Lawrence, provided "a *coup d'oeil* hardly surpassed on earth,"[1] and where the precarious perch on Table Rock afforded an overwhelming view of Niagara, one of the natural wonders of the world.

Some scenes mingled elements in what an 1844 writer called "a glorious perversion of geography."[2] Tropical animals framed views in Canada's frozen north; palm trees were absurdly flung round a view on the St Lawrence. But this "perversion of geography" is in itself interesting: it provides insight into nineteenth-century attitudes. The Victorians believed, with William Henry Bartlett, that topography had the power to make every country an object worthy of attention, but they did not hesitate to improve on the reality of geography (art, in the opinion of one critic, was almost under an obligation to idealize, "for this is only completing what Nature begins").[3] Many Victorians embraced with ease an eclecticism that was a mingling of incongruities.

Wares with Canadian views must be set against the background of the potting industry. Printed earthenware was the foundation on which British potters of the nineteenth century built up an export trade that was the envy of their competitors in other nations. The Canadian views are part of a vital chapter in ceramic history.

Some Canadian views were from what the Canadian importers liked to call "the first potteries of Staffordshire" (such as Enoch Wood's well-known manufactory); others came from potters in business in a smaller way (Thomas Godwin of Burslem, for example); still others were made in Scotland. The people who bought their products were those who wanted useful wares both decorative and sturdy.

Transfer printing, as a Victorian writer observed, did "almost as much for British pottery" as the art of printing itself "did for literature."[4] Picture pottery became a ceramic fashion of the nineteenth century, widely demanded, widely produced. In all the welter of designs and patterns that underglaze printing made possible the topographical view assumed a special place. The "best landscapes" on pottery, said a critic writing in the *Art Union* in 1844, were "those taken from published prints."[5] The potters' views of Canada are part of a rich and fascinating heritage.

CHAPTER ONE

Printing on Pottery

"... for sale ... printed ware ... now so generally used."
Royal Gazette (Halifax), 13 March 1811

British-made earthenware with printed decoration was the most popular of all the ceramic wares used in nineteenth-century Canada. It was in demand not only in Canada but around the world. What a contemporary commentator called the "untiring," almost "savage" intensity of British industry was epitomized in these ceramic products made possible by the mastery of mass production that was the direct outcome of the Industrial Revolution.[1] It is with this class of ceramic wares that earthenware printed with Canadian views belongs. Its makers were potters in England and Scotland.

When compared with the potters of the Orient and continental Europe, the British had come late to world markets. Only in the second half of the eighteenth century did they begin to press their older rivals. Their initial success was based on a cream-coloured earthenware whose decoration was most often hand-painted. At the end of the century a French scientist, Faujas de St Fond, noted the impact of English creamware. "Its excellence," he said, had won it "a commerce so universal" that at every European inn "one is served with English ware. Spain, Portugal, and Italy are supplied with it, and vessels are loaded with it for the East Indies, the West Indies, and the continent of America."[2]

Faujas de St Fond was writing in the 1790s. By the beginning of the Victorian period another French scientist, himself a potter, was again noting what the English were doing and again singling out their earthenware, but now it was earthenware whiter in appearance and with underglaze printed decoration that was to the fore. "The English," admitted the French potter, "surpass all other nations ... in printing."[3]

In the nineteenth century this printed earthenware pushed creamware aside and took its place as the chief ceramic export of Great Britain. The thrusting ascendancy of printed wares was conspicuous before the first decade of the century was out. In 1809 a writer in Ackermann's *Repository of Arts* took stock of the British potting industry and observed that the manufacturers who were "calling in the aid" of the engraver were "giving to their country a new source of beneficial commerce." While the porcelain makers were still engaged in "making ... progress to an equality with other countries" the earthenware potters, with their firm grasp of new techniques, were producing wares whose "superiority is universally acknowledged and is particularly attested by the vast quantities which are continually exported to every quarter of the globe."[4] Some thirty years later another writer in another English magazine summed up succinctly the place of printed earthenware: "in the whole range of ... pottery manufacture, there is no kind of decorative operation which has been more generally approved."[5]

There were two methods by which a design could be transferred from an engraved copperplate to a piece of pottery: by means of bats (or slabs) of a glue-like substance (bat printing), or by means of specially prepared paper tissues. It was the second method, the one normally implied whenever transfer printing is spoken of, that was employed by the potters who produced views of Canada. Bat printing gave delicate effects and was used to a limited extent by some of the leading potters of Great Britain, but it was a slow process, and was used more often for printing on (not under) the glaze and for work on porcelain rather than earthenware. The more robust underglaze printing, effected by means of the paper tissues, was the method best suited to a fast-paced industrial age which saw Britain's ceramic exports leap up from a total worth of £573,000 in 1840 to £2,500,000 a year in the next decade.[6] The potters' views of Canada, with decoration printed under a protective glaze (ensuring durability) on an earthenware body that varied in quality (something to suit every pocket), were part of a great outpouring of sturdy wares for everyday use.

A number of contemporary accounts described the transfer printing process. One of these appeared in 1832. In the 1830s some of the most attractive of the Canadian views were being produced. The description as given in Rev. Dionysius Lardner's Cabinet of Useful Knowledge tells not only how these wares of Canadian interest received their decoration, but would have been how Canadians of the day understood it. Lardner's "useful knowledge" series was popular in Canada and was available in such newsrooms and libraries as the library of the Mechanics' Institute of Montreal, an institute founded in 1828 and which published a catalogue of its library some years later.

In the words of this 1832 account:

> The method of transferring printed designs to earthen vessels is thus pursued. The landscape or pattern is engraved upon copper [Plate 1], and the colour, which is mixed with boiled linseed oil, is laid on the plate in the same manner as ink is usually applied by copper-plate printers. To increase the fluidity of the oil, the plate is then temporarily placed in a stove, a sheet of damped tissue paper is laid on it, and both are passed in the ordinary manner through the press [Plate 2]. The paper, wet with colour, is then delivered to a girl, who reduces its size by cutting away the blank

portion surrounding the pattern, and passes it to another girl, by whom the impression is applied lightly to the ware when in the state of biscuit. A third girl is next
employed, who with a piece of woollen cloth, rolled tightly in the form of a cylinder,
rubs the paper closely against the piece, in order to press the colour sufficiently into
its substance. The paper thus rubbed is left adhering to the article for an hour, when
both are placed ... in water, so that the paper becomes soft enough to be peeled off ...
having transferred to the biscuit the impression which it had received from the
copper-plate.

When the pieces thus printed have stood a sufficiently long time to become dry,
they are placed in an oven, to which a gentle heat is applied, in order, by dissipating
the oil, to prepare the wares for receiving the glaze ... For a long time blue, produced
from the oxide of cobalt, was the only colour employed; but, of late, the potters have
extended to this pleasing branch of their art all the colours on their palette.[7]

At every stage there were factors to be watched. The temperature of the copperplate was important; the tissue paper had to be laid against the pot with precision;
otherwise wrinkles in the paper or careless joining of parts of the design were evident in
the finished product. Over the years improvements took place – in the paper, in the
mixing of the colours – but the basic steps outlined by Lardner were those followed to
the end of the century by the makers of earthenware printed with Canadian scenes.

Underglaze transfer printing was not a nineteenth-century invention. Contrary to
what is generally stated, it may not even have been an English one.[8] It was first used on
porcelain, not earthenware. But regardless of when it was first used or by whom, it was
the nineteenth-century earthenware potters of Great Britain who exploited it to the full
and made of it a "universally acknowledged" source of "beneficial commerce." At the
end of the eighteenth century, underglaze transfer-printed earthenware was waiting in
the wings, ready to play a central role on the nineteenth-century stage.

How soon and how quickly printed earthenware became part of the ceramic trade
of Canada may be traced in documents and printed sources. One of the earliest
Canadian references to it occurs just before the dawn of the nineteenth century in the
business papers of a spectacularly successful Quebec City merchant. George Pozer
counted among his business contacts the fur trader John Jacob Astor and Lord Nelson's
friend and executor Alexander Davison; he held contracts for provisioning the garrison; he acquired seigneuries, and at one time owned the famous Chien d'Or hotel.
Among his multifarious enterprises was general merchandising, with a strong emphasis
on crockery.[9]

In 1798 Pozer was approached by a ship's captain from Liverpool with a selection
of earthenware from the newly established Herculaneum Pottery. An exacting
businessman, Pozer complained at once about the way the earthenware had been
packed, but he found it, none the less, "of good quality," saleable in Quebec. He
proceeded to deal directly with the pottery. On 27 October 1798, he wrote to Samuel
Worthington, proprietor of Herculaneum, ordering a long list of tablewares to be
dispatched in the spring of 1799, when the ice would be out of the St Lawrence and

Quebec freed of its winter isolation. It was a foretaste of things to come that this 1798 order from Canada included a small lot of "Blue printed" earthenware, one of Herculaneum's products from the outset.[10]

Although in 1798 "Blue printed" formed only a small part of what the sharp, money-making Pozer ordered (the bulk of his order, as would be expected at this date, was for creamwares), the presence of "Blue printed" in any quantity is significant. From this point on, the evidence of its acceptance in Canada mounts quickly. One year after the writer in Ackermann's *Repository* was commenting on the growing dominance of printed wares in the export trade, Joseph Frobisher, the great Nor'Wester, was buying printed earthenware from John Shuter in Montreal. On 26 July 1810, Shuter, another of the chief merchants of Lower Canada, sold Frobisher printed tablewares to the value of twelve shillings.[11] That printed earthenware was on its way to being firmly established in the Canadian trade very early in the nineteenth century is confirmed by a Halifax advertisement of 1811. On 13 March that year Edward Alport announced a shipment of "blue printed ware"; then he added these words: "now so generally used."[12]

Blue, as Lardner stated, was the first colour used successfully on a broad commercial basis for underglaze printing on earthenware. It was the first colour that could be depended upon to withstand the heat of the glost (or glaze) oven. For this reason, the process was long known as "blue printing," even after other colours had been mastered. William Evans, a former pottery worker who described the process in 1846, began his account by saying: "*Blue printing* is the name for the manipulations of taking impressions (in colours, blue, green, pink, and brown,) from copper-plates."[13]

These other colours had begun to make their appearance with increasing frequency on the Canadian market by the beginning of the 1830s, just about the time Lardner was speaking of the potters' command of "all the colours" on a palette. In New Brunswick, Richard Calvert of Saint John was advertising "fancy coloured printed Earthenware" in 1834;[14] in the Eastern Townships of Lower Canada, W.W. Smith of Missisquoi Bay was selling "black printed teas ... in sets" in 1835;[15] in Upper Canada, Shriver and Dean of Bytown (Ottawa) had "DINNER AND TEA SETTS" in "Blue, Pink, and Brown" in 1836 (in their general store, where they also sold furs and groceries).[16] Earthenware with Candian views was to appear in all these colours.

The closing years of the eighteenth century saw the printed wares creeping in, hesitantly ordered at first in small lots by Canadian importers who were trying them out against older wares of proven sales appeal. By 1811, as Alport's Halifax advertisement shows, the printed wares were drawing even (his advertisement offered the "blue printed ware" in company with other earthenware whose decoration, on what was probably a creamware body, was simply a brown-painted edge). By the 1820s printed earthenware was dominant, its place unchallenged from then on as the tableware most commonly found in Canadian homes.

Printed earthenware dominated the market for one compelling reason: it was suited to the times that produced it. From the lively days of the Regency through decade after decade of an energetic Victorian world a restless, relentless striving after change and variety gripped the public. At mid-century Digby Wyatt, the English architect and first Slade professor of fine arts at Cambridge, aptly summed up the age when he spoke of a constant "panting" for "striking variation."[17] Potting was a highly competitive business; any potter who hoped to stay in it had to give the public what it wanted. In one brief sentence the *Illustrated London News* stated the potter's position in this breathless world of change. What "the people *will* have," said the *News* in 1851, "... [the] manufacturer *must* make."[18] The manufacturer (or potter) had to provide variety, not just for the home market but for markets overseas. The importers' annual lure in Canada, when the first spring shipments arrived from the British potteries, was "new patterns just out this season."[19]

The semi-mechanical process of underglaze transfer printing was a vital means by which nineteenth-century British potters secured their place in a new world of industrialization. The full force of this world struck the French critic and historian Hippolyte Taine as almost terrifying. In the 1860s he stood at a Thames-side wharf and noted the frenetic activity: "bales are always being piled up, sacks being hoisted, barrels being rolled, cranes are creaking, capstans sounding."[20] It was a world which a Canadian, Canniff Haight, described in 1881 as having "jumped from change to change with marvellous rapidity."[21] Throughout the century printed earthenware "jumped from change to change" with the "marvellous rapidity" needed to give a voracious public new colours, new patterns, new styles.

The population explosion which had accompanied the Industrial Revolution provided the potters with an expanded market in Great Britain itself; the resulting waves of emigration which swept over the ocean and into colonies such as Canada provided an expanding market abroad, a market concerned with goods for "all Society's less'ning grades" (as a Canadian versifier put it in 1866).[22] Underglaze transfer printing enabled the potter to inundate the markets with wares ranging from the frankly cheap (hurriedly done printing on the cheapest body possible) to wares whose added gilding on a well-potted body satisfied a taste for show. Aggressive marketing methods on the part of importers pushed the attractions of printed earthenware. Buyers in St Catharines in 1831 were assured that blue, brown, and "fancy" printed earthenware ranked as "prime" goods.[23] In Edmonton, in the days when Alberta was still part of the Northwest Territories, "Fancy Printed Tea Sets" from Great Britain were advertised enticingly "At prices never before heard of."[24] It is against this background and as part of this setting that earthenware with Canadian views must be placed.

CHAPTER TWO

The Death of Wolfe

"... this picture will ... occasion a revolution in the art."
Sir Joshua Reynolds, 1771

Intense public interest in what has been described as the most popular military print in the history of art prompted the earliest of the Canadian views on earthenware.[1] In the eighteenth century it caught the attention of the foremost potter of the day. Almost half a century later nineteenth-century potters were still making use of the same theme. This early view was not topographical but a death scene: the death of General James Wolfe, on 13 September 1759 at Quebec. The leading potter to make use of it was Josiah Wedgwood. The unprecedentedly popular engraving was William Woollett's "Death of Wolfe," after Benjamin West's painting (Plate 4). The painting itself, from which the engraving was made, is now in Ottawa in the National Gallery of Canada.

The English porcelain makers had been the first to seize upon military and naval heroes of the Seven Years War (1756–63). From Bow and Worcester came commemorative items. Bow produced an impressive standing figure of Wolfe (paired with the Marquis of Granby, who had distinguished himself in the European theatre of the war).[2] Worcester turned out commemorative mugs with portraits of Wolfe, Granby, and Admiral Edward Boscawen ("Old Dreadnought," who commanded the fleet at the siege of Louisbourg in 1758, the year before the battle of the Plains of Abraham).[3] It was, however, the powerful effect of West's painting and the engravings after it that gave a subject from the Seven Years War its widest distribution; and it was earthenware potters, not porcelain makers, who capitalized on the long-lasting popularity of a Canadian historical scene.

To understand the impact of West's painting and all that followed from it, it is necessary to remember what a bold departure from convention this British American artist had chosen. West, born in Pennsylvania when it was British territory, was already an established historical painter in London at the time he undertook his "Death of Wolfe" in 1770. The death of a military hero whose life had been snatched from him at the very moment of victory had stirred the public in a way scarcely matched in British history. Poets, authors, artists had burst into tributes to Wolfe. West was attempting a subject already dealt with by others. He made a decision that his friends thought astonishing and unwise: he decided to paint the figures in modern military dress, thereby flouting the convention of portraying heroic scenes with figures in classical costume. He was not the first, but he was one of the first and by far the most influential to make this break with artistic tradition.

When West's intention became known, none other than Sir Joshua Reynolds, president of the Royal Academy (a position West was to hold before the century was out), tried to dissuade him. Sir Joshua's arguments were reinforced by the Archbishop of York, Dr Robert Drummond. Both men pointed out to West the vulgarity of painting heroes in coats, breeches, and boots such as anyone might see worn on the street any day of the week. West persisted. When his "Death of Wolfe" was exhibited at the Royal Academy of 1771 it was a startling, instant success. Sir Joshua capitulated: "Mr. West has conquered ... I retract my objections ... I foresee that this picture will not only become one of the most popular but occasion a revolution in the art."[4] The public saw it as a great moment in history powerfully captured, and in a form that was still a novelty.

West's painting overshadowed anything that had gone before. An earlier (1764) rendition of the same scene by a minor artist, Edward Penny, also with figures in modern dress, was historically more accurate. West's version was full of inaccuracies. He introduced officers not present when Wolfe died (some said he did so for a price); he included the picturesque detail of "a noble savage," but there were no Indians with the British forces.[5] The inaccuracies did not matter to a public captivated by a scene rendered with West's dramatic vigour. Not only was his "Death of Wolfe" engraved, West himself had to paint replicas, including one for King George III. The original painting (the one now in Ottawa) was purchased by Lord Richard Grosvenor, the king having failed to secure it through a misunderstanding.

The painting had been an instant success; William Woollett's engraving of it, published on 1 January 1776, made it known to almost everyone. Thousands of copies were sold. It made a fortune for Woollett and an even greater fortune for John Boydell, the publisher, who obtained full ownership of the plate after Woollett's death in 1785. Potters were less likely to have been inspired by a painting than by an engraving (a medium nearer to their own and one which reached a wider market). It was more likely, then, to have been Woollett's engraving than West's actual painting which first caught the eye of the makers of earthenware. The greatest potter of them all, Josiah Wedgwood (1730–95), rarely went to London without hunting in the print shops for subjects for his creamware (called by him "Queen's Ware" after Queen Charlotte began using it in the 1760s).

Woollett's engraving went on sale in the London print shops in 1776. It was about two or three years later that the "Death of Wolfe" began making its appearance on such Wedgwood items as teapots and jugs. When a published engraving was taken up for pottery decoration, some changes had usually to be made. There would hardly have been room on a piece of pottery for all the figures West had included in that death scene. It was, therefore, the central group and the figures to the right only that were used on this creamware (Plate 3).

Historians are not in agreement as to who, or even how many, were present at the moment Wolfe died. As an eighteenth-century account put it, "many, from a vanity of talking, claimed the honour."[6] West's flagrant inaccuracies confused the issue still further. Modern scholarship now disputes even certain of the identifications previously accorded figures painted in by West. As the scene appeared on Wedgwood, a surgeon (his identity a matter of debate) kneels by the dying Wolfe, attempting to stay the flow of blood from the fatal wound. Other officers kneel to the left or stand behind Wolfe. The officer with the flag is usually accepted as Lieut Henry Brown (or Browne), "of the Grenadiers of Louisbourg and the Twenty-second Regiment," who wrote to his father, some weeks after the battle, that "The General did our company the honour to lead us in person, as he said he could depend upon our behaviour, and I think we fully answered his expectations."[7] The most arresting figure among the officers is the Louisbourg Grenadier at the extreme right. He stands wringing his hands in anguish, the wind of that cold September morning blowing his hair. Beside him, his hands also clasped, is Wolfe's servant.

It is testimony to the popularity of this dramatic engraving that Wedgwood used it on articles intended for general sale and special orders both, combining it with totally unrelated scenes and inscriptions. Usually printed in black, but sometimes in sepia, it appears on jugs and teapots printed on the reverse with "Success to the INDEPENDENT VOLUNTEER SOCIETIES of ... IRELAND"; it appears on jugs with an English rural scene, on others with a shipping scene, and on teapots and jugs with "Success To the ... EARL of DERBY." Private collections in Canada and such public collections as those of the National Museum of Man in Ottawa, the Royal Ontario Museum in Toronto, and the New Brunswick Museum in Saint John all have examples of these wares, most of them with the mark WEDGWOOD impressed. The jug in the National Museum of Man has the Irish nationalist sentiment on the reverse and, under the spout, the initials of the original owner.

The printing on these items was not done at Wedgwood's pottery in Staffordshire but in Liverpool. Early in the 1760s Wedgwood had entered into an arrangement with the Liverpool printers, John Sadler and Guy Green, to execute work for him on his creamware. Sadler retired from the partnership in about 1770 and Green continued the business alone. Printing, with the exception of some outline work for such items as crests, was not done at Wedgwood's in Staffordshire until after the death scene at Quebec was first produced. Precise dating, however, of these Wolfe items is difficult and their dates may vary. With regard to the Liverpool printing, it is generally assumed that the work of Sadler and Green was always on, not under the glaze, but a check of examples in the Wedgwood museum at Barlaston indicates this may not invariably have been the case.[8] The later years of the eighteenth century were still early days for transfer printing on earthenware and there remains something yet to be learned about the products of that period.

English potters other than Wedgwood made use of the same group of figures from the "Death of Wolfe." In the 1890s Joseph and Frank Kidson, in their history of the Leeds Pottery, claimed it was one of the printed subjects found on eighteenth-century creamware from that important manufactory.[9] An unmarked mug in the City of Liverpool Museum is also ornamented with the scene, printed in black. In this case the ceramic engraver was not the firm of Sadler and Green but Thomas Rothwell, who signed the engraving ("Rothwell Sculp"), and who may at that time have been working for one of the early creamware potters of Liverpool.[10] William Turner, writing on transfer printing in 1907, recorded an unmarked jug printed in purple with the "Death of Wolfe" in the collections of the Victoria and Albert Museum in London.[11]

The death scene was reproduced not only as printed but as moulded decoration by earthenware potters working at the end of the eighteenth and the beginning of the nineteenth centuries. Plaques moulded in low relief were produced in several sizes, the figures touched with colours in the distinctive palette that characterizes what are loosely termed Pratt wares. Just where all these unmarked plaques originated is not known, but potters in both England and Scotland did this type of work.[12]

The makers of stoneware provide still further evidence of the continuing interest in the scene as painted by West and engraved by Woollett. Herculaneum, the Liverpool pottery founded in 1796 and for which George Pozer of Quebec and Edward Alport of Halifax both became agents, made use of it as relief decoration on jugs that are in date c. 1800–10.[13] Samuel Hollins, a Staffordshire potter, used it on a buff stoneware of about the same date.[14] It turns up, too, on unmarked black basaltes teaware.

When the news of the capture of Quebec and the death of General Wolfe reached England in October 1759, there was, according to an old account, a "sort of mournful triumph."[15] Though bonfires roared into flames as word spread from town to town throughout the land, something of the poignant drama of those last moments on the Plains of Abraham filtered down even to the crowds in the streets. It was this chord that West managed to touch and which Woollett's engraving brought home to thousands. Historians might carp that nothing could be more absurd than to call West's work historical; the public was given what it wanted, not only by the artist and the engraver but by the potters.

In the 1820s the death scene at Quebec appeared once more, this time as under-glaze printed decoration in blue on the whiter-appearing earthenware that had pushed cream-coloured ware aside. The body to which Josiah Wedgwood had given the name "Queen's Ware," and which had most often been ornamented with hand-painted decoration or, if printed, had usually received that printing on top of the glaze, was replaced as the best-selling ware in Britain, Europe, "and the continent of America" by earthenware whose decoration wore better because it was printed under the glaze – and printed more effectively against a background white rather than cream in colour.

The blue-printed version of the death of Wolfe was not the scene as West had painted it for an admiring public in the eighteenth century. It was a stilted, artistically inferior, and even more inaccurate picture that Jones & Son, an obscure Staffordshire firm, used as part of a multi-scene pattern entitled "British History." The wares carried an ornate printed mark on the back, combining the maker's name, the general pattern

FIGURE 1
Printed mark, Jones & Son

---

name, and the title of the scene on that particular piece (Figure 1). "Death of General Wolfe" was the title of the picture on large meat dishes (or platters). These dishes were offered in two forms: flat-bottomed, as in the example from the National Museum of Man (Plate 5), or of the well-and-tree variety (described in the nineteenth century as dishes with "little ditches" to conduct the gravy to "a well at one extremity").[16] The scene appeared also on the pierced, flat inserts (strainers) that went with some of the dishes.

Jones & Son's "Death of General Wolfe" included a figure of an Indian (standing, not kneeling as in West's painting, and which had been omitted entirely by the cream-ware potters). There was, too, a touch not even West had attempted to introduce. Behind Wolfe loomed a horse and rider. There were no Indians, there were no horses on the British side of the battlefield when daylight broke on 13 September 1759. Scaling the heights of Quebec in the dark had been a gruelling task for the British troops. Persuading horses to make the climb, and that silently, had been no part of their plan.

There were many versions of the death of Wolfe, some painted and engraved by continental artists. The pottery engraver who executed the work for Jones & Son may have had a published source (or sources) from which he worked, or he may simply have drawn upon his own imagination. Other subjects in the "British History" pattern included the signing of Magna Charta, the death of Lord Nelson, and the Battle of Waterloo. The border used on the series was suitably composed of patriotic symbols and emblems (the crown, roses, thistles, shamrocks) and military trophies.

The "British History" pattern belongs to the 1820s. One of the events chosen (and used on soup tureens) was the coronation of King George IV, which took place on 19 July 1821. Although the exact year when Jones & Son began business is not certain, their "British History" pattern was obviously not introduced until after George IV came to the throne. He died on 25 June 1830. Little loved and even less respected, his coronation would have been considered an occasion worth recording as a memorable event only close to the time it took place. Jones & Son, in any case, seem to have been out of business before the decade was over.[17]

These eighteenth- and early nineteenth-century wares depicting the death of Wolfe at Quebec are among the earliest of all the potters' views relating to Canada. They record an event that was not only a turning point in Canadian history but one that was to have important results for the potters themselves. Even before the Seven Years War was officially over and the treaty of Paris signed in 1763, British wares had begun to make their way into the newly acquired colony of Canada. In its issue of 6–8 August 1761, the *London Chronicle* reported that British goods were now "in the greatest plenty" in Quebec. The British potters had a new and, for many years, a protected market thrown open to them at the very moment when the industry was on the threshold of development, and when they were readying themselves to make their first determined bid for a place in the front rank of the world's potters.

CHAPTER THREE

Canadian Scenes from the "Father of the Potteries"

"... his manufacture embraces almost every ... article
required by the Trans-Atlantic Markets ..."
Simeon Shaw, 1829

On the morning of 16 December 1829, the Staffordshire pottery town of Burslem awoke to the firing of cannon, the ringing of bells, and the blare of band music. That night the whole place was "one blaze of light." In the words of the *Staffordshire Advertiser* the next day: "A general illumination took place, as if by magic ... The Town Hall was brilliantly illuminated and several appropriate transparencies were displayed in the windows of different inhabitants." This general rejoicing was not, as might be supposed, the celebration of some great military victory or national event. Instead, as the *Advertiser* explained, it was "one of the most disinterested, unsought, and flattering compliments that was ever paid to an individual moving in private life" – a celebration, moreover, that ended decorously, "unclouded either by accident, riot, or disorder."[1]

The potters had turned out to honour one of their own. Enoch Wood (described that same year as the "venerable Father of the Potteries")[2] was celebrating his fiftieth wedding anniversary. His business in 1829 was flourishing, bringing prosperity to the district (Plate 6). With his sons, he had built up what was reckoned the largest North American trade in earthenware of any of the Staffordshire potteries.[3] Included in this vast flood of exports – thousands of articles in a single shipment – were tablewares with underglaze transfer-printed views of Canada: Table Rock at Niagara, Quebec City, and Montmorency Falls, six miles below Quebec. Today these blue-printed scenes are considered among the most striking and desirable of all the potters' views of Canada. The National Museum of Man has examples of all three views in its collections.

On that same December day in 1829, when Enoch Wood's workmen were being regaled with refreshments and the poor of Burslem were queuing up for free soup handed out in honour of the golden wedding, a shop on Montreal's St Paul Street, down near the waterfront, was taking orders for the firm's products. William Peddie had advertised in the *Montreal Gazette* only a few weeks earlier that he had received "a sett of Samples" from "ENOCH WOOD & SONS OF STAFFORDSHIRE." He stood ready to furnish "Prices Current" and "terms of payment" to "Importers of CROCKERY."[4] Representing Enoch Wood in Montreal meant that Peddie, one of the city's prominent merchants, was the agent for one of Staffordshire's most respected potters.

It was not just his age (he had been born in 1759, the year of the battle of the Plains of Abraham), nor the fact he was a large-scale employer (in 1833 his employees numbered over a thousand), that won Enoch Wood acknowledgment as the "Father of the Potteries." What won him "disinterested, unsought, and flattering compliments" was his tireless interest in the business of potting and his native town of Burslem. He had secured improvements for the town, had contributed generously to the building of St Paul's church, had served in civic capacities, and was celebrated both as a local antiquarian and as a modern manufacturer.

The man who ornamented tablewares with the grandeur of Canadian waters and the majestic heights of Quebec was a member of a noted potting family. The son of Aaron Wood (the block-cutter and modeller) and the nephew of Ralph Wood (the first of the figure-makers of that name), Enoch Wood had begun business in the 1780s. In 1818 he took three of his four sons (Enoch, Joseph, and Edward) into partnership (Plate 6). It was during this partnership that the Canadian views were produced. Though their father died in 1840, the sons continued the business under the old style of Enoch Wood & Sons until 1846.

The exact date when the Canadian views were introduced has not been determined, but the general appearance of the wares and the colour of the underglaze printing suggests it was towards the end of the 1820s or the beginning of the 1830s. The richly dark cobalt blue used for these Canadian scenes is, for many collectors, one of their chief attractions. It is a colour that seems to have appealed strongly to the North American market of the day, judging by the amount of earthenware printed in it for export, not only by Enoch Wood and his sons but by other Staffordshire potters as well. One of the first Canadian references to wares in this colour occurs in a Montreal newspaper, the *Canadian Courant*, on 30 October 1824. On that date S. & W. Spragg announced that their recent importations included:

> 10 Crates Dark Blue Earthenware,
> 50 Boxes Tin and Sheet Iron ...
> 3 Cases Women's and Men's Shoes.

There was nothing unusual about tablewares being jumbled together with hardware and boots in Canadian shops of the 1820s; what is noteworthy about the *Courant* advertisement is the particular mention of "Dark Blue." One of Enoch Wood's eccentricities provides further evidence that dark blue was favoured at this period. The "Father of the Potteries" had a penchant for burying examples of his current productions and one place where he deposited a large cache was in the foundation walls of St Paul's church in Burslem (the church to whose building fund he had contributed £100). The corner-stone was laid in 1828. In 1974, when the church was demolished, over three hundred pieces of Enoch Wood's earthenware came to light, among them nineteen decorated in the characteristic dark blue for the American market.[5]

The nineteen pieces had views of the United States, not of Canada.[6] Yet these American views help to date the Canadian, because Enoch Wood's Canadian views were made as part of a long list of North American subjects intended for sale to customers in the United States. The firm made sales to both Canada and the United States of "almost every ... article required by the Trans-Atlantic Markets."[7] These sales included vast supplies of earthenware whose decoration had nothing at all to do with North America. What William Peddie was advertising in Montreal in 1829 was almost certainly earthenware with decoration of this general kind. Enoch Wood, however, made a conspicuous effort to woo the United States with American views. More than five dozen appeared on earthenware from his pottery. The three Canadian views were part of his American series, intended for a market that was larger and more rewarding than Canada's.

Curiously, one of the three Canadian scenes was for almost a hundred years classed by American writers as an actual American subject. Even those writers who conscientiously separated Canadian from American subjects fell into the trap. Annie Trumbull Slosson was one of the first to list Table Rock as a view in the United States. Writing in 1878 under a pseudonym ("The Youngest Member") she published a now rare and entertaining little book called *The China Hunters Club*. She devoted a chapter to "American History Illustrated in Pottery." Some of the dark blue printed wares, she noted, "are superb in colour, and although once cheap crockery, they are now valuable specimens whose worth consists in their great beauty of colour as well as in their historical associations."[8] She made no mention of Canadian views, listing only American and including Table Rock.

In 1892 Alice Morse Earle, whose *China Collecting in America* is equally evocative of the Victorian "china mania," made her own list of American views and mentioned Canadian scenes. She placed Table Rock in the American section and stated that Quebec and Montmorency Falls were "the only views of Canadian scenery" known to her "on old Staffordshire."[9]

The error went on. Dr Edwin A. Barber was "the recognized authority" on "historical pottery" at the turn of the century.[10] In 1899, in *Anglo-American Pottery*, he included Table Rock in company with such American scenes as the Capitol at Washington and Mount Vernon (both by Enoch Wood & Sons). In a separate section for Canadian views by the Woods he listed Quebec and Montmorency Falls.[11] Fifty years later Ellouise Baker Larsen was still placing Table Rock with American subjects. She, too, had a category for "Canadian Views by Enoch Wood & Sons," with Quebec and Montmorency as the only listings.[12]

This strange anomaly was corrected in 1967 in *Nineteenth-Century Pottery and Porcelain in Canada*.[13] It is difficult to see how it could have persisted for so long. It was one thing for Enoch Wood & Sons to produce Canadian scenes that would have sales appeal in the United States; it is quite another for a Canadian scene to be listed as an actual American view, particularly when Quebec and Montmorency Falls were set apart as Canadian. Although both the United States and Canada claim a share of Niagara Falls themselves, the location of Table Rock was always indisputably on the Canadian side of the border, and any ceramic view so entitled can be accurately classed only as a Canadian subject.

In the nineteenth century Niagara was regarded as one of the miracles of nature. An overseas visitor of the 1840s described the incredible sheet of water as "like the beautiful robes falling from the shoulders of a goddess." This same visitor, Rev. James Dixon, a Methodist minister from England, viewed the falls first from the American side, then crossed to Canada. Hurrying towards Table Rock, "the usual and best position to obtain a perfect view," he was suddenly struck by the truth and exclaimed aloud: "We are on the territories of Queen Victoria. Pull off your hat!" He doffed his hat "in reverence to the majesty of England," then hastened on to Table Rock.[14]

An American journalist, writing in 1847, suggested a novel way to view Niagara: from beneath Table Rock. Those who would experience "emotions of awe and sublimity" were advised to lie on their backs at the base of the rock and from this position gaze upwards.[15] Awe and sublimity were emotions people of sensibility expected to feel in the presence of nature's more magnificent manifestations.

The intense interest in Niagara resulted in countless numbers of pictorial representations. Enoch Wood chose a particular aspect: a view with Table Rock high up at the right overlooking the splendour of the Canadian scene (Plate 7). The source he used was an engraving in a book published in St Petersburg (now Leningrad) in 1818 (Plate 8). The author was Paul Svinin, a Russian who had been in North America in the early years of the century. The engravings in the book, entitled (in translation) *A Picturesque Voyage in North America*, were after water-colours by Svinin himself.

Table Rock had been so named because it projected beyond the cliffs that supported it, "like the leaf of a table."[16] Over the years portions of it broke off and hurtled down into the rushing waters below. It became increasingly hazardous for tourists to use it as their vantage point. "The remaining portion of Table Rock may fall at any moment," wrote Isabella Bird in 1856.[17] On 16 July 1867 the Montreal *Gazette* reported that "The greater part of the table-rock is separated from the mainland by a space of several inches in width ... presenting a very dangerous appearance." Later that same month massive charges of gunpowder were used to blow up the rock: "The sight was very grand."[18] It is understandable why Enoch Wood chose Table Rock for one of his North American views. As the Rev. James Dixon said, it afforded a "dazzling" scene; appropriately its own end was spectacular.

Niagara was not the only Canadian waterfall to strike those who saw it with a sense of awe. In the opinion of John Long, a fur trader and Indian interpreter who served with the Loyalist forces during the American revolutionary war, Montmorency Falls, higher and narrower than Niagara, was "perhaps the most pleasing natural cascade in the world."[19] Benjamin Silliman, professor of chemistry at Yale, saw Montmorency in 1819; and just as the Rev. James Dixon had compared the waters of Niagara to the robes of a goddess, so Silliman likened Montmorency to "the drapery" of "Grecian statues."

FIGURE 2
"Table Rock" mark, E. Wood & Sons

Montmorency, he wrote afterwards, was so well known by description that any traveller might feel prepared for the view, but when confronted with it, the sight was transcendently glorious and "beyond ... expectations."[20]

Enoch Wood's source for Table Rock is known; the source for what was entitled on the back of the wares FALL OF MONTMORENCI has yet to be discovered. According to Mrs Larsen, the "View ... most nearly resembling the one used by Wood is W.H. Bartlett's *Montmorency Cove ...* published in *Canadian Scenery*."[21] This cannot be correct. There are at least three reasons why Bartlett must be dismissed out of hand as either the source or the inspiration for the Wood view: there is no resemblance to Bartlett's style (the view of Montmorency by Wood quite evidently belongs to an earlier period); the actual articles of tableware on which the view appears are almost certainly earlier than the 1840s (the earliest possible date for Bartlett to have been the source); the presence in the Wood view of an observation house (the little building seen high up and to the left, jutting out over the waters) rules out Bartlett completely – it was a building Bartlett never saw and never could have seen (Plate 9).

The little summer or observation house was erected in 1792 by Sir Frederick Haldimand, the governor of Quebec. It was described three years later by an English visitor, Joseph Hadfield, who recorded in his diary that an awesome view of "the greatest and most distinguished part of the falls" could be obtained from the "small temple" hanging over the immense precipice and "supported by stays of wood from rocks below."[22] The "small temple" was precariously perched. Before the end of the century visitors were examining with alarm the rotting stays of wood. John Cosens Ogden, an American tourist who drove out from Quebec to gaze at Montmorency in

FIGURE 3
Marks, E. Wood & Sons

1799, observed that the "decays of time" had spelled its doom.[23] It was gone before the 1830s, when Bartlett came to Canada. At a later date another structure was erected, but by that time Enoch Wood & Sons were out of business.

Niagara seen from Table Rock and Montmorency viewed from Sir Frederick's "small temple" struck seekers after the picturesque as among the finest sights of the world. Quebec City was another irresistible attraction. Hadfield, catching his first sight of it from the water, took one look at the walled city towering above him, and the prospect around it, and declared the sight "the most sublime, grand and varied" he had ever beheld.[24]

Benjamin Silliman was more impressed with Quebec as a fortress, an aspect Enoch Wood's view immediately conjures up, showing as it does the resemblance of Quebec to Gibraltar, "the fortress rock of the Mediterranean" (Plates 10, 11). Many visitors called Quebec the fortress rock of the St Lawrence. Silliman felt Quebec was the most impregnable town in North America, "and one of the strongest in the world."[25]

As with the view of Montmorency Falls, Enoch Wood & Sons' source for their picture of Quebec has not yet been found. It may well be that both have a common origin in some traveller's account, even as the view of Table Rock was taken from Svinin's *Picturesque Voyage in North America*. All three Canadian scenes were of places tourists invariably tried to see. This was the reason they were included by the Woods in their series of North American views produced with the American buyer in mind. Americans were travellers in the nineteenth century, just as they are today. To many of them Table Rock, Montmorency Falls, and Quebec City would have had as much familiar appeal on a dinner table as the Hudson River scenes or the views on the Passaic

FIGURE 4
"Quebec" mark, E. Wood & Sons

that were featured on other Enoch Wood & Sons' tablewares with the same shell border and in the same dark, brilliant blue.

The mark used on both the Canadian and American views is conclusive evidence of the market the Woods had in mind. This printed mark featured prominently the American eagle, shield, and motto: E PLURIBUS UNUM. The title of the scene was also part of the mark: TABLE ROCK / NIAGARA (Figure 2); FALL OF MONTMORENCI / NEAR QUEBEC (Figure 3); QUEBEC (Figure 4). An impressed mark, again with the American symbols, often accompanied the printed one and included the makers' name (E. WOOD & SONS / BURSLEM) and indicated the type of earthenware body used (SEMI CHINA).

No potter designing wares specifically for the Canadian market would have used American symbols that were at the time repugnant to Canadians, or a motto that was to Canadians menacing in its meaning, "one out of many." In the 1820s and 1830s there were still those who could remember the days of the American revolutionary war, when American armed forces had crossed the border, seized Montreal, and attempted to take Quebec. Even more recent was the War of 1812, when Americans had again invaded Canada. For many years after the conclusion of that war in 1814 border incidents continued to erupt, threatening further hostilities. Benjamin Silliman, during his visit to Quebec in 1819 had been able to pick up an American newspaper there containing a provocative comment on how easy it would be, should the need arise, to take Quebec City "*at the point of the bayonet.*" Silliman remarked that such inflammatory words did little to help keep the peace and that it would, in any case, be as rational to talk of taking the moon as to speak of storming the defences of Quebec.[26]

The fact that these Canadian scenes were intended in their own day for sale in the

United States, as the marks used on them clearly show, does not now detract from their interest for the Canadian collector. The scenes are Canadian, from a famous pottery that had its own Canadian links. They are essential in any collection that illustrates the potters' view of Canada.

Although Alice Morse Earle stated that entire dinner services with the view of Table Rock were exported to America,[27] it is almost always plates that collectors now come upon; and it is on plates that the view of Montmorency is also found. Quebec City occurs on both tea and dinnerware. In the collections of the National Museum of Man there is a handsome covered dish with Quebec on the interior. Around the outside and on the cover are American scenes (or sections of them): West Point Military Academy, Lake George, and the Highlands, Hudson River.

The Canadian views chosen by Enoch Wood & Sons are prime examples of the type of topographical view admired in the early nineteenth century. They embody the sense of transporting emotion, the gush of feeling which the sublime in nature inspired. Taste and emotion had been trained to respond vehemently to a sense of the overwhelming, the awe-inspiring, as in great heights and tumbling waters. Niagara, Montmorency, and Quebec met every requirement. Nothing in the Old World or the New produced greater sensations of feeling.

CHAPTER FOUR

Potters and Paddle-Wheelers

"No wind or tide can stop her."
Quebec Mercury, 6 November 1809

The age that looked to nature to inspire "lofty sentiments ... of majesty and glory"[1] worshipped also the achievements of man; and none of man's achievements in the nineteenth century inspired livelier excitement on the part of the general public than the taming of wind and tide by steam power. "No wind or tide can stop her," exulted the *Quebec Mercury* (6 November 1809) on the arrival in port of the first steamboat to ply Canadian waters. That first Canadian steamboat was the *Accommodation*, built in Montreal for John Molson, the brewer, who now threw himself enthusiastically into the promotion of steam on the St Lawrence. So important did this aspect of Molson's varied business life become in the eyes of the public that a French-Canadian curé, writing him for a parish loan some years later, addressed the request simply to "Monsieur Molson, Bourgeois des Steamboats, Montreal."[2]

The role played by steamboats on inland waters and later by steamships battling Atlantic gales to set new records for ocean crossings was a sensational part of the jumping from change to change "with marvellous rapidity" that Canniff Haight of Toronto spoke of in 1881 as the hallmark of the century.[3] Inevitably the advent of steam caught the attention of potters who, in their turn, jumped from change to change in order to keep afloat in their own world of business.

The earliest and by far the rarest of any of the potters' representations of steamboats associated with Canada is fittingly connected with the Molson line. The first mention of tablewares carrying a picture of a paddle-wheeler identified as belonging to the St Lawrence Steamboat Company (the name eventually adopted for the Molson line) appeared in 1933 in B.K. Sandwell's history of the Molson family.[4] In 1955 Merrill Denison, in another history of the Molsons, again referred to tablewares bearing "a side-view" of a Molson steamboat.[5] Both Sandwell and Denison implied that Molson family tradition held the steamboat to be the *Accommodation*. Denison accepted it as such, but this identification is inaccurate. The steamboat as depicted on unmarked tablewares from England bears a much closer resemblance to later Molson paddle-wheelers. Sandwell, in fact, pointed out a significant discrepancy between the *Accommodation* and the steamboat on tableware. On tableware the paddle-wheels are completely boxed in. The *Accommodation* had open paddle-wheels. Among the illustrations in both books is a picture of an "early" Molson steamboat (not the *Accommodation* but perhaps the *Malsham*, launched in 1814) which is remarkably like the steamboat recorded by the unidentified potter.

Tablewares with the picture of this steamboat, and with the name of the St Lawrence Steamboat Company on a banner over her, cannot be earlier than 1822 and are probably not later than the beginning of the 1830s. In April 1822 what was popularly known as "the Molson line" became a joint stock company under the name St Lawrence Steamboat Company. (On tablewares, the name is spelled "St Laurence," a not uncommon spelling of the day.) The majority shareholders, charged with the management of the company, were John Molson and his sons. The exact date when the name ceased to be used is less certain. In 1833 the St Lawrence Steamboat Company and the Tow Boat Company (belonging to the Torrance family) were merged. The newly formed company advertised under the name of the St Lawrence and Montreal Tow Boat Company,[6] but it is possible the old name (St Lawrence Steamboat Company) continued to be used on occasion, at least for a time. The few existing examples of earthenware with the picture of the paddle-wheeler are themselves the best guide to their date. They have the appearance of the 1820s or, at the latest, the very early 1830s. Sandwell's comment, again evidently based on Molson family tradition, that the tablewares were "credited to the year 1825" is entirely compatible with their appearance.

Sandwell spoke of "dinner plates" (presumably in family possession); Denison of a single plate "in faded lavender colours" which, he said, was in the Château de Ramezay, Montreal. A thorough search of the Château's collections on three separate occasions has failed to turn up the plate. The known examples are in blue, and any colour other than blue remains to be confirmed. Denison stated that John Molson himself designed the pattern for this tableware and that there was a service of it aboard the *John Molson* (launched in 1827). He cited no authority for his statements and it is unlikely that Molson designed a pattern. Molson may have provided a sketch of one of his paddle-wheelers. He may even have suggested the patriotic symbols (roses, shamrocks, thistles) which surround the steamboat, but it is highly improbable he was responsible for the actual pattern into which this steamboat has been set.

On finely potted earthenware, the steamboat is pictured with paddles furiously churning the waters. Smoke billows from her twin funnels, calling to mind the "huge" boats "with double chimneys" which a Scottish visitor to Montreal observed in 1818 (a year when several Molson steamboats were hurrying up and down the St Lawrence).[7] The name of the company floats on a banner over her. The patriotic symbols surround her (Plate 12). The whole is incongruously set into a pattern of Old World buildings and garden flowers. The overall border is composed of the garden flowers linked by stylized foliage. It is a pattern and border the English potter would almost certainly have had in production at the time he received the order from Canada.

What little information there is about the wares associated with Molson, the "father of the steamboat enterprise in Canada," leaves some questions unanswered. It is not clear whether they are from a service ordered by Molson and possibly used by him aboard one of his steamboats, or whether these were wares used in serving meals to passengers. If they were for the travelling public aboard Molson boats, then they differ markedly from most of the earthenware made for later Canadian steamboats and steamships. Usually wares of this kind carry only a crest or a name of a shipping company or, if decorated with some conventional pattern (such as the "Willow" pattern, used on Allan liners in the 1880s), have the company's name printed on the back (not the face) of the wares.

Whatever its original use, this earthenware with its view of a paddle-wheeler is of special interest today. To the collector, it represents a great rarity in Canadiana; to the historian, it is a tangible reminder of how extraordinarily early Canada was propelled into the age of steam. John Molson's first steamboat, the *Accommodation*, splashed down the St Lawrence only two years after Robert Fulton, the American pioneer, had launched his steamboat on the Hudson. She was toiling up and down the St Lawrence three years before the first commercially successful steamboat in Europe (the *Comet*) was operating on the Clyde. Admittedly, Molson's *Accommodation* had her performance limitations, but she takes her place as one of the first commercial steamboats in the world, the herald of steamboating on one of the world's greatest rivers.

With characteristic energy John Molson followed up his bold entry into modern transportation with newer, more powerful, more commodious steamboats. His *Swift-sure* ("equal to the best hotel in Canada"), *Malsham* (probably the boat depicted on tableware), *Lady Sherbrooke*, and *New Swiftsure* were all in service within ten years.

As would be expected, Molson had competition in what was obviously going to prove a lucrative business. The age of steam transportation began at the time when immigrants from the British Isles were starting to pour into Canada. They arrived in their hopeful hordes at the port of Quebec. Most of those who came to this part of Canada were on their way to what is now Ontario. "They set this way in such o'erwhelming floods, Canadians! take your last look at the woods" was the cry of a Kingston newspaper in 1820.[8] Conveying immigrants up the St Lawrence to Montreal, where they would enter upon the next stage in their long, wearisome journey to a new home in a new land, was a money-making proposition. Only a few of the ocean-going ships were able, at this time, to make their way past Quebec. The channel between Quebec and Montreal was shallow and tortuous, and such ocean vessels as attempted it generally avoided the risk of running aground by transferring part of their cargo to "lighters" as they neared Montreal. Steamboat proprietors seized opportunity in two ways: they provided passenger service, and they provided towing service. James Strachan, visiting Canada in 1819, was quick to note that "the prosperity of the steam vessels" was fast becoming "the ruin of all the sloops and river craft," and although he half sighed for the fate of the older craft, he confessed that he preferred the new mode of travelling: "The ease of travelling by steam-boats is so very great."[9]

John Molson was the pioneer in the development of St Lawrence steamboats, but members of the Torrance family soon emerged as powerful competitors. It was a Torrance steamboat, the *British America*, that provided one of the most important potting firms of the day with a Canadian subject. The *British America* was built in Montreal in 1829 and went into service on the St Lawrence in 1830. Her portrait, with Montreal as a backdrop, appeared on earthenware made in Staffordshire at the pottery established by John Davenport in 1794. Unlike the tablewares featuring a Molson steamboat, there is no uncertainty concerning the use of these Davenport wares: they were made for sale to the general public; they were not a special order of any kind, nor were they for use aboard the *British America* herself.

The Davenport view was adapted, with certain significant alterations, from an engraving published in 1830. Robert Sproule, an Irish artist who had emigrated to Canada, advertised in the *Montreal Gazette* on 12 November 1829 that he proposed "*publishing* a set of SIX VIEWS" of Montreal. They were subsequently issued by Adolphus Bourne. Sproule was the artist; Bourne, owner of a Montreal engraving establishment, the publisher; W.S. Leney, whose name appears erroneously on the published views as "W.L. Leney," the engraver.

One of the views was entitled "View of Montreal From Saint Helens Island," and it was this view, with a borrowing from another, that Davenport adapted to pottery decoration (Plate 13). The name chosen for the pattern was "Montreal." The pattern name is usually printed on the back of the earthenware (Figure 5); usually, too, the impressed Davenport mark of the firm's name over an anchor is present (occasionally the name may be printed, not impressed).

Although Davenport called the pattern "Montreal," and although its inspiration was obviously the engraving published by Bourne, there are certain changes which indicate plainly that the pottery engraver also drew upon some additional source. It was, of course, usual for pottery engravers to make changes when adapting a published view. A number of such changes were made in this case: the sentry and sentry box on St Helen's Island (a garrison post) have, for example, been dropped; the steamboat has changed direction (on earthenware she is heading upstream, not downstream, as in the published view); a raft has disappeared but a canoe, taken from another of the engravings in the series, has been added (Plate 14). There are more than half a dozen changes of this kind. The most significant are in the steamboat in the foreground. On earthenware the steamboat has been brought into much greater prominence than Sproule gave her; the position of her paddle-wheels has been changed; most important of all, she has been given a name. In neither Sproule's original water-colour (now in the McCord Museum of McGill University), nor in the engraving as Bourne published it is the steamboat identified. There were, in 1829, a number of steamboats she could have been. The boat on Davenport earthenware is emphatically identified as the *British America*: in large letters on the side, on a pennant, and with the initials BA on a flag (Plates 15, 16).

FIGURE 5
Davenport marks

What additional source of information was put at the Staffordshire engraver's disposal, prompting him to depart in such a striking manner from the published engraving, is a question that may never be conclusively answered. There is, however, evidence to suggest that Adolphus Bourne himself may have provided the information. The clue lies in Bourne's own background, and in the fact he was on a business trip to England in 1832 when the *British America* was a new steamboat, much in the news.

Adolphus Bourne, who came to Montreal in 1820, was a Staffordshire man, born there about the end of the eighteenth century.[10] In Staffordshire history the name Bourne is associated with both potters and copperplate engravers. "The Bournes are a very ancient potting family," said an 1870s account,[11] and according to Staffordshire directories there were Bournes potting in the district in the 1790s, 1820s, 1840s, 1860s. In 1818 one of the most important engraving workshops in the Potteries was Bentley, Wear & Bourne. In Montreal, Staffordshire-born Adolphus Bourne combined both engraving and pottery interests. He had arrived in Canada as an engraver;[12] in the 1840s, while still carrying on his engraving business, he became an importer of earthenware and porcelain.[13] Even earlier he may have been connected, either directly or indirectly through his family, with the firm of Bourne & Wright who were advertising in the 1830s that they would supply Montreal crockery dealers with "every description of this article" from Staffordshire at the lowest wholesale price.[14] Given the biographical facts, plus the information that Bourne was actually in England not long after both the launching of the *British America* and the publication of the views of Montreal,[15] it then becomes distinctly possible that any supplementary suggestions for this Davenport view could have come straight from him. It is likely – even probable – that Bourne was in

Staffordshire visiting his relations on that 1832 trip overseas, a trip undertaken in connection with his engraving business.[16]

The earliest possible date for Davenport's "Montreal" is about 1832; more likely it was introduced somewhat later. It took time to bring out a new pattern, even when all the material for a pottery's engraver to work from was at hand. There is no evidence, in any case, that Davenport's printed patterns were engraved at the factory itself. Outside engravers, such as the well-known Bentley, Wear & Bourne (who continued under various partnership changes over many years),[17] were responsible for much of the work which appeared on Staffordshire printed wares. Bourne's contact in Staffordshire – if there was one – may have been with a ceramic engraving firm which subsequently provided Davenport with the design. Bourne was, after all, an engraver himself.

The existence of examples of Davenport's "Montreal" printed not in mono-chrome but in multi-colour (blue, green, brown, and a pink tinged with purple, all on the same piece) suggests a date around the mid-1830s, at least for the multi-colour version. It is known that Davenport was doing work of this kind in the second half of the 1830s. Terence Lockett, the authority on Davenport, has written of a plate printed in multi-colour with a scene from Sir Walter Scott's novel *Waverley*, which has a date mark for 1836;[18] and Geoffrey Godden some years ago recorded a Davenport dinner service in a multi-colour pattern described in the original bill of sale as "Colored Muleteer," with a factory date mark for 1835.[19]

Specimens printed in multi-colour, their border divided into compartments containing pink floral sprays against a brown background, are the rarest form of this potter's view of Canada. Most of what the collector will find will be in monochrome printing. The choice, however, is wide: pale blue, pink, brown, grey, lavender, or black. On the monochrome-printed wares the border is composed of flowers linked by scrolls below a narrow chain design with pendant dots.

In dating these wares it is a point to note that in the mid-1830s monochrome printing in colours such as pink and brown and what was advertised as "light blue" (paler than the blue normally used at the beginning of the century and only a faint relation of the brilliant "dark blue" used by Enoch Wood and his sons) became increasingly popular with Canadian importers. The "light blue" was frequently particularized at this period, just as the "dark blue" had been specified as something new and fashionable in the 1820s. One country storekeeper who not only stocked the new pale blue but also offered to take farmers' produce in exchange for it was W.W. Smith of Missisquoi Bay, in the Eastern Townships of Quebec. In the summer of 1835 Smith advertised "Light blue printed dining ware, in sets ... PRODUCE of all descriptions ... taken in payment."[20]

The fact that the Davenport view shows the two towers of Notre Dame church rising against the Montreal skyline should not be taken as an indication that the pattern must be dated after the 1840s, when the towers were completed. Sproule, in 1830, depicted Notre Dame as it was planned and it so appeared in his "View of Montreal From Saint Helens Island." Another of the six views in the series showed Notre Dame as it really was in 1830, without the towers.

Davenport's "Montreal" must have been in production over a number of years. The amount of it produced, the range of colours, and the pattern's widespread distribution all point in that direction. Examples have turned up in Canada, the United States, Mexico, Portugal, Spain, and in Great Britain. This is not surprising. Davenport was a heavy exporter to many parts of the world, with agents in European cities and with trade connections responsible for huge shipside sales in Canada.[21] A pattern entitled "Montreal" and featuring a modern steamboat satisfied two of the prominent interests of the period: the glamour of faraway places and the equal glamour of scientific progress. It had special appeal in Canada; elsewhere the appeal was general.

The *British America* was one of the most admired of the St Lawrence steamboats, renowned as both a passenger and a tow boat. Lady Aylmer, wife of the governor-in-chief of Canada, described her in 1831 as "very fine ... with every convenience."[22] The power of her engines permitted her to take three merchant vessels in tow at the same time. In Lady Aylmer's eyes she was "immense." She would readily have fitted into John Duncan's category of huge steamboats with double chimneys. As Davenport pictured her, she was battling the treacherous St Mary's Current which flows between Montreal and St Helen's Island, a current that the earliest steamboats had been unable to get up on their own. The *British America*'s fame lasted to the end. On Christmas Day 1850 a *Montreal Gazette* advertisement, offering her engines for sale, recalled her "speed and power ... so well known."

In their "Montreal" pattern Davenport made all manner of dinner and dessert ware, including hot water plates, and baskets with pierced sides (such as the basket and stand in the collections of the National Museum of Man). The firm, in existence for almost a century (1794–1887), was capable of top quality work. The earthenware on which the pattern was printed was consistently well potted, the printing itself usually well executed, the colours attractive in their light, delicate tones.

While extremely desirable in any Canadiana collection, Davenport's "Montreal" is not so rare as another potter's view also inspired by and this time closely following the engraving of Montreal published by Bourne. This version, recorded only so recently as 1981,[23] is by an as yet unidentified potter. It occurs in brown or blue underglaze printing and appears to date in the mid-1830s or early 1840s (Plate 17).

In this little known view, entitled on the back VIEW OF MONTREAL, the steamboat is unidentified, her paddle-wheels are placed where Sproule sketched them, and she is no longer the dominating feature of the scene. She heads downstream, as in the original water-colour and engraving from it (Plates 18, 13). The raft, dropped from the Davenport view, has returned. The leafy tree, whose position was shifted by Davenport, remains unaltered on the left of the picture. In short, this potter's view is much closer to the published engraving. At the same time, there are departures from the published engraving which this second potter's view shares with the Davenport scene, immediately suggesting some link between them. Both views, for example, include the canoe. The interpolation of the canoe cannot be explained simply by saying the unidentified potter copied Davenport. His inclusion of features taken from the published engraving but not found in the Davenport scene is evidence that the engraver working for the unidentified potter had before him Bourne's "View of Montreal From Saint Helens Island" (Plate 13). Even the title of this second ceramic view ("VIEW OF MONTREAL") is closer to Bourne's title. A possible, but speculative explanation of the relationship between the two potters' views might be that the same engraving establishment provided both designs. It was common practice for Staffordshire engraving firms to work up different versions of the same scene to sell to different potters. The Davenport view has a spirited quality lacking in the second potter's production, but engraving firms, such as Bentley, Wear & Bourne, often employed a number of workmen, each of whom would interpret the material in his own manner.

The border on the "VIEW OF MONTREAL" is distinguished by vignettes of tropical palm trees alternating with small sailing craft. The palm trees, unsuitable as they are to the St Lawrence, are explained by the fact that this Canadian view was part of a multi-scene pattern which included a number of West Indian scenes, possibly taken from James Hakewill's *Picturesque Tour in the Island of Jamaica*, published in 1821.[24] In this pattern the Montreal view appeared on tureen stands. It may have been used on other articles yet to be discovered.

Canadian enterprise was very much to the fore in the history of steam transportation. An Englishman who arrived in Canada in 1819 looked in astonishment at the St Lawrence steamboats: "there are no vessels of the kind in the world superior to them," he exclaimed.[25] In 1834, when the *British America* was a dominating presence in the river traffic, another arrival from overseas declared that "to view nature and steamers on a truly grand ... scale" it was necessary to come to the St Lawrence.[26] "Magnificent" was the succinct summing up of St Lawrence steamboats by the son of a British prime minister.[27] The initiative that spurred men like John Molson and his sons and John and David Torrance provided Staffordshire manufacturers with subjects that today are among the most historically interesting of all the potters' views of Canada.

CHAPTER FIVE

Viewing the Cunarders

"... what is a steamboat crossing the Atlantic ... but a miracle?"
James Dixon, 1849

The potters' involvement with Canadian advances in steam transportation did not end with the Molsons and the Torrances. In 1840 Samuel Cunard of Halifax (Plate 19) became the first to span the Atlantic with a fleet of wooden paddle-wheelers carrying the royal mails and committed to regular schedules. At least three potters celebrated this feat on earthenware.

At the beginning of the Victorian period the British government was considering ways to speed Empire communications. Steam was the answer. When tenders were called for replacing the Halifax sailing packets with steamships, Cunard won the contract. The brash colonial's success surprised everyone. Rivals were contemptuous. They said he had nothing to offer except plans; but his plans were breathtaking: to provide ships that would criss-cross the Atlantic, departing and arriving "with the punctuality of railway trains on land."[1] Fortunately for Cunard, he had friends as well as enemies. An influential one had proved to be Sir William Edward Parry (whose earlier exploits in the Arctic also inspired pottery decoration). In 1837 the Admiralty had become responsible for the Post Office packets, and Parry was in charge of this aspect of the Admiralty's work. He not only befriended Cunard when, in 1839, the Novascotian was awarded a £60,000 contract; he later stood by him when certain modifications of the contract became necessary.

Securing the mail contract was the first step, but Cunard still had to find money to build the ships needed for the awesome task ahead. Again he was aided by overseas supporters, mainly by shrewd Scotsmen, who enabled him to form the British and North American Royal Mail Steam Packet Company. It began service in 1840 with four wooden side-wheelers: *Britannia, Acadia, Caledonia,* and *Columbia.* On 4 July the *Britan-*

nia inaugurated the service. She sailed from Liverpool, her paddle-wheels labouring deep in the water under the enormous weight of the coal she carried to stoke her voracious engines. (With these early transatlantic steamers speed increased as the voyage lengthened and the coal diminished.) Twelve days and ten hours later the *Britannia* was in Halifax. Two days more and she docked in Boston, the western terminus of the route.

Statistics vary concerning the first Cunarders, built on the Clyde and fitted with engines by Robert Napier, but a contemporary Canadian advertisement, giving the names of the famous four under contract with "the Lords of the Admiralty," claimed they were 1,250 tons and 440 horsepower each. They berthed 115 passengers, but not cheaply: it was $125 from Liverpool to Boston, "exclusive of Wines."[2]

On both sides of the Atlantic tremendous excitement was engendered by this latest evidence of scientific progress. Even Charles James Mason, the flamboyant Staffordshire potter who patented the name "Ironstone China" for a tough earthenware, and who had a marked preference for oriental-type patterns, was caught up in it. He brought out a design featuring a handsomely printed picture of the *Britannia*. Reginald Haggar, who has examined such Mason pattern books as still exist, has made the interesting discovery that this particular design must have been prepared well in advance, when it was still uncertain which of the Cunarders would lead the way. The terms of Cunard's contract required the four ships to be ready by approximately the same date. At the time Mason decided on a view of a Cunarder, it had yet to be announced which ship would sail first. The pattern book shows an unnamed steamship with a space for her name to be filled in.[3] When Mason's design was offered for sale, the *Britannia*'s name was there.[4] Framed with marine symbols, she appeared on a plate whose outside border harked back again to the oriental. That Mason would be ready and waiting to commemorate Cunard's achievement is an indication of the immense interest in this latest evidence of Victorian enterprise. Plates have been recorded with this design, but other articles may have been produced.

Mason was probably the first to celebrate the Cunarders and he appropriately chose the *Britannia*. The next away was the *Acadia*. She sailed from Liverpool on 4 August and clipped thirty hours off *Britannia*'s time. Throughout her career she maintained a reputation for speed. It may have been this which prompted another British potter to use her in his response to public interest. Since the earthenware with the pattern name "Acadia" has no maker's mark, the potter remains unidentified. The pattern name, however, printed within a garter device that surrounds a steamship, is usually present (Figure 6).

As with Mason's *Britannia* design, the "Acadia" pattern featured a steamship dramatically framed, this time within an exuberant inner border with elements of the baroque. The outer border was boldly stylized with prominent palmettes. The potter used earthenware of an ironstone type but not approaching Mason's in quality. The pattern was offered in underglaze transfer printing in a harsh blue or in mulberry (a blackish purple much favoured in the later 1840s and in the 1850s).[5] The colours were usually what were described in Canadian advertisements as "flowing" or "flown," giving

FIGURE 6
"Acadia" pattern mark

the blurred or misty look admired in North American markets. Dinner, tea, and toilet wares were all produced, with gilding occasionally added to rims and handles (Plate 20).

Perhaps more than any of the other patterns brought out when the first Cunarders were making news, the "Acadia" had a good sale in Canada. There is, for example, evidence that the prominent Toronto china merchant, James Jackson, was stocking it. The proof lies in examples of this pattern with his name on the bottom, printed within a wreath:

J. JACKSON
IMPORTOR [sic]
TORONTO

The pattern has the appearance of the later 1840s. This is confirmed by the fact sugar bowls printed in it are identical in shape to a bowl in a private collection (in a flowing blue floral pattern) which has the name of the Montreal importers Glennon & Bramley. Glennon & Bramley were in business together from 1842 to 1847 or the early part of 1848. Jackson, the Toronto importer, was advertising actively in the 1850s, but was probably in business earlier, judging by other wares that carry his name.[6] It is possible, on the other hand, that the "Acadia" pattern was in production longer than one would have supposed and that old shapes were used.

Charles James Mason chose the *Britannia*, the unidentified potter the *Acadia*; a pair of Staffordshire brothers, James and Thomas Edwards, made use of all four of the first Cunarders. They called their pattern "Boston Mails," emphasizing, in this case, the

FIGURE 7
Mark used by J. & T. Edwards

American link with this Canadian-inspired project. The pattern, a multi-scene one, was registered on 2 September 1841. The main decoration showed the interior arrangements of the ships: the ladies' cabin (Plate 21), gentlemen's cabin (Plate 22), the saloon, all with passengers serenely engaged in such pleasant occupations as reading, taking refreshment, doing needlework, or simply having conversation with fellow passengers. The pattern was offered on tea, dinner, and toilet wares and in both multi-colour and monochrome printing (brown, black, pink, lavender, or light blue). The pattern name, printed above a steamship, and information concerning the registration were on some of the wares, with or without the maker's name (Figure 7). Most often the steamship device and pattern name appeared alone.

The border was sometimes omitted, particularly on the wares printed in black, but when present, the border displayed pictures of the ships. (Plate 23). Exact portraits were not intended, even though the ships were usually named. These representations show, however, that each of the Cunarders was equipped with sails as well as paddle-wheels. To many a traveller, timidly trying out the new, fast means of ocean crossing, the sight of the sails billowing out in a stiff Atlantic breeze was reassuring. The Rev. M.B. Buckley, an Irish priest who came to Canada on a Cunarder (to raise money for Cork cathedral) was glad to see this familiar form of power brought into auxiliary use early in the voyage. In his diary he wrote: "we hoist sails, and the vessel looks more important in her full dress."[7] With paddles digging into the ocean and canvas spread to the wind, Cunarders kept to their pre-arranged schedules, slashing days and weeks from the travel time of sailing vessels.

It is reasonable to suppose that the "Boston Mails" was based on published views of some kind. The source has not yet come to light. Charles Dickens, who booked passage on the *Britannia* in 1842, en route to a lecture tour in Canada and the United States, spoke of a series of lithographic views which were hanging in "the agent's counting-house in London,"[8] but these may have been the lithographic sheets, part advertisement and part accommodation booking plan for foreign or British coastal paddle-steamers (not ocean-going vessels), which are in date c. 1836, and of which there are examples in the National Maritime Museum in London.[9] One cannot entirely dismiss, however, Dickens' tantalizing references to "highly varnished" views showing a "spacious" saloon and fashionably furnished cabins in which "groups of passengers" were depicted "in the very highest state of enjoyment" (Plate 24).[10] Unfortunately, he himself had a rough crossing, was seasick, and wrote later that those lithographic views had vastly exaggerated the pleasures of life aboard a steamer, but he did admit to some pleasant moments around the fireplace in the ladies' cabin. (A fireplace is seen in some of the views of the ladies' cabin on the Edwards' wares.)

A much more enthusiastic passenger was the Rev. James Dixon from Liverpool who made his voyage to Canada aboard the *Acadia* six years later. He described her as "a beautiful vessel, well fitted up with a fine and spacious saloon above deck."[11] It is Dixon's account of a transatlantic crossing by steam that furnishes an insight into the impact Cunard made upon the public, an impact that inspired Staffordshire potters to bring those early steamships to the dinner table. Dixon had an even more boisterous crossing than Dickens, and for some days the *Acadia* made slow progress, but that she made any progress at all seemed to Dixon remarkable proof of the "mechanical" genius of man. "Nothing," he wrote, "gives so striking an illustration of the wonderful effects of steam-power as progress made in such circumstances. The waves were constantly rolling against us; driven by a mighty swell ... increased ... by the accumulated impetus of storms, current, tides ... and yet we made way against this combination of adverse elements. We ... beat nature in a battle with her mightiest forces. How amazing this power! ... We decry miracles; what is a steamship crossing the Atlantic, in the midst of opposing powers, but a miracle?[12]

As long as those first four Cunarders were adding a new dimension to the history of transportation there was a sale for them on earthenware. They represented to the public an aspect of life in which the Victorians had supreme confidence: the power of man through science to command unending progress.

The *Britannia* and the *Acadia* lasted until the end of the 1840s. They were sold in 1849 to the North German Confederation. The *Caledonia* was sold to the Spanish government in 1850. Only the *Columbia* came to grief. She was wrecked on 2 July 1843 on a rocky ledge off Seal Island, some miles from the Nova Scotia coast. In spite of this disaster (the ship was beyond repair), Cunard kept to his contract with the Admiralty. The moment the news reached him in Halifax, he dispatched a smaller steamer, not normally used as a passenger liner, and sped the mails to England on time. Neither a life nor a letter was lost.[13]

The rarity of the Mason's wares with the picture of the *Britannia* would indicate they were produced in small quantity and probably at the very beginning of transatlan-

FIGURE 8
Marks used by J. Edwards

tic service. The appearance of the wares with the unidentified potter's "Acadia" pattern suggests they were still in production at the end of the decade and they may have been carried on longer. The Edwards' "Boston Mails" has traditionally been given a very brief life span. Most writers have attributed it exclusively to the firm of James and Thomas Edwards, who registered the design in the autumn of 1841. Since the brothers dissolved partnership soon afterwards (Llewellynn Jewitt gives the date as 1842) that would mean the pattern was only in production for perhaps a year.[14] In 1967, in *Nineteenth-Century Pottery and Porcelain in Canada*, the possibility was raised that James Edwards, who potted on his own account for almost ten years after the partnership with Thomas was terminated, might have continued the "Boston Mails."[15] The amount of it to be found and the appearance of much of it, particularly of some of the wares printed in black and without the border, indicated a date later than 1841 or 1842. That possibility has now become a fact and the over-all dating of these wares must be revised. The collections of the National Museum of Man include at least one plate, borderless and black-printed with a view of the gentlemen's cabin, marked with the usual steamship device and pattern name but which has, as a maker's mark, the impressed initials of James Edwards alone (Figure 8). This places it after the brothers ceased potting together and before 1851, when James took his son into partnership (their marks included the initials J. E. & S.).[16]

All these wares (Mason's, the unidentified potter's, the Edwards') were made for general sale. They were not made for use aboard the steamships themselves. These are wares that represent the potters' response to a Novascotian's enterprise. When Cunard died on 28 April 1865, he was proclaimed "the best friend of ... progress in the whole history of navigating the ocean by steam power."[17]

CHAPTER SIX

Arctic Scenery

"... the death-like stillness of ... desolation ..."
Edward Parry, 1821

It was inevitable that the potters' views of Canada would include Arctic scenery. Throughout the whole of the nineteenth century polar regions that are now part of Canada were in the news in one way or another. In the Regency and the opening years of the Victorian period it was the almost mystical quest for the Northwest Passage, linking Europe and Asia through the seas and channels of the Canadian north, that caught the imagination of the public. During the rest of the century the haunting search for Sir John Franklin and his men, who had sailed off into the Arctic mists in 1845, gripped the attention of Great Britain and North America alike. The search for the elusive passage that would connect the Atlantic and the Pacific Oceans and the search for the lost explorers, who had been looking for it, were often the same thing. It was while looking for Franklin that a British naval officer, Robert McClure, found the Northwest Passage in 1850.

Names of Arctic explorers became household words on both sides of the Atlantic. The published accounts of their discoveries, with engravings from drawings taken on the spot, were among the most popular travel books of the day, often running to several editions. A new edition of one of Edward Parry's voyages was selling in a Montreal bookshop in 1834,[1] a date that puts it very close to the time when scenes adapted from his works were printed on tableware.

Not only were their books read in Canada, some of the best known of the explorers had ties with the older, settled parts of the country. Parry had been in Halifax as a naval officer during the War of 1812. His recollections of those days contributed to his friendly attitude towards Samuel Cunard when, years later, Cunard sought his help in securing an Admiralty contract for carrying the mails to Nova Scotia. Franklin, returning from two years in the Canadian north, arrived by canoe at Bytown on a summer's

FIGURE 9
"Arctic Scenery" pattern mark

evening in 1827. The next day he laid the first stone of the locks of the Rideau Canal, watched by "as large and respectable a gathering of spectators" as had ever been seen in the future capital of Canada.[2]

The sustained and excited interest in the Canadian Arctic was turned to his own advantage by a British potter who produced a multi-scene pattern entitled "Arctic Scenery." No maker's mark seems to have been used, but the pattern name, printed on the back of the earthenware within a device composed of an igloo set against towering ice peaks and flanked by harpoons and a standing figure, is usually present (Figure 9).

The pattern was printed underglaze in blue, pink, brown, or green. The views, which appear on the various articles of dinnerware (plates in several sizes, meat and vegetable dishes, tureens, etc.), were loosely based on illustrations found in two of Parry's works: *Journal of a Voyage for the Discovery of a North-West Passage From the Atlantic to the Pacific; Performed in the Years 1819–20 in His Majesty's Ships Hecla and Griper* (published in London in 1821), and *Journal of a Second Voyage for the Discovery of a North-West Passage From the Atlantic to the Pacific; Performed in the Years 1821–22–23 in His Majesty's Ships Fury and Hecla* (published in 1824). The pottery scenes are composites (Plate 25), with bits and pieces put together from a number of the engravings illustrating the *Journals* (Plate 26). More than half a dozen different scenes have been recorded in the ceramic series; there may be more.

The pottery engraver drew not only on the illustrations in Parry's works but also on his own inventiveness – or else he made use of some additional and as yet unidentified source of polar views. In, for instance, the scene on a large meat dish belonging to the National Museum of Man, inhabited tents in a winter setting appear

(Plate 27). The illustrations in Parry's *Journals* show no such tents, although in the *Journal of a Second Voyage* there is an illustration entitled "Summer Tents of the Esquimaux." The "summer tents" occur in a virtually snowless landscape and differ considerably from those on earthenware.

On the whole, there is a stilted quality to the potter's "Arctic Scenery" not characteristic of the illustrations in the *Journals*. Parry's illustrations were from sketches made by some of the officers who accompanied him; the engravers, when it came time to publish text and illustrations, included the talented William Westall, ARA, and Edward Finden, who shared with his brother William a reputation for engraving noted for fine finish. The work of these engravers had a sophisticated quality that the pottery engraver, working with the contrived scenes, was unable to transmit.

The stilted manner of the pottery scenes is nowhere more evident than in the view found on both dinner and soup plates made up from two of Parry's illustrations (Plate 28). From the *Second Voyage* come the Eskimos and dogs in the foreground, adapted from "Sledges of the Esquimaux" as sketched by Capt. F.W. Lyon and engraved by Finden (Plate 29). From the first *Voyage* come the all-important sailing ships, adapted from "H.M. Ships Hecla & Griper in Winter Harbour," drawn by Lieut F.W. Beechey and engraved by Westall (Plate 30). The ships on earthenware give but a thin idea of the dramatic quality of the original engraving. The pottery scene may best be described as having an attractive and, it must be admitted, somewhat confused naïveté. The published illustrations achieved at times a solemn, brooding power.

Parry himself spoke of the sombreness of polar scenery: scenery which had "more of melancholy than of any other feeling."[3] What Parry called "the death-like stillness" of "desolation" was captured in illustrations such as Beechey's "Hecla & Griper in Winter Harbour." The ships on tableware are toy ships, far removed in spirit from the bomb-vessel *Hecla* (built with massively strengthened fore-part to withstand the tremendous weight and the recoil of mortars mounted in wartime) and the gun-brig *Griper* (rigged as a barque for the polar voyage). As Beechey depicted them, they create the impression of the warriors they were, ready to pit their strength heroically against the might of Arctic ice.

The confusion of the potter's views of the Canadian north is heightened by his choice of border. Even the best of Staffordshire's potters sometimes combined central views with incongruous borders. A certain amount of incongruity might be expected, but the "Arctic Scenery" border carries it to the extreme. These scenes amid snow and ice, in a land where even in summer the cold might be so intense that the sea would remain frozen solid, have been encircled by lush garden flowers and tropical animals.

Yet outlandish as the "Arctic Scenery" border is, it is an important aid in dating the introduction of the pattern. A number of the animals in the panelled border were taken from *The Naturalist's Library*. This series of well-illustrated little books, edited by Sir William Jardine, comprised forty volumes brought out between March 1833 and July 1843. The inexpensive size of the volumes, the hand-coloured illustrations, the treatment of the subjects, all contributed to their continuing appeal, calling for a number of editions. They were frequently advertised in Canada. In 1861 the whole set, with "1200 coloured plates," was advertised in Montreal as among the most desirable literary importations from overseas.[4] The lion (Plate 31) and ocelot in the "Arctic Scenery" border come from a volume first published in February 1834. Unlike most ceramic borders, the one used with "Arctic Scenery" is not always exactly the same: the parade of unsuitable creatures featured in it may vary.

The evidence of the border sets the earliest possible date for "Arctic Scenery" as the mid-1830s, a date that accords well with the general appearance of the earthenware, although it may be that the pattern slips into the beginning of the 1840s. The second half of the 1830s and the beginning of the 1840s was a period in which both explorers and public alike were possessed by the dream of a passage which all believed existed but none could find. Accounts of Arctic explorations streamed from publishers' presses. Everyone read them, in cheap or costly editions. Some of the leading potters of the day subscribed to handsomely illustrated volumes detailing the latest discoveries. In 1835 that veteran of the search for the Northwest Passage, Sir John Ross (who had extricated himself and most of his gaunt and tattered men from a gruelling ordeal), published his *Narrative of a Second Voyage in Search of a North-West Passage and of a Residence in the Arctic Regions during the Years 1829, 1830, 1831, 1832, 1833*. Subscribers to the two-volume edition with coloured plates (there were other editions) included W.T. Copeland, the Staffordshire potter and London alderman, a member of the Davenport family from Staffordshire, and J.D. Pountney, one of the leading Bristol potters.[5] A year later (1836) another naval officer, George Back, who had been sent out from England to look for Ross, published his Arctic discoveries; that same year Dr Richard King, the surgeon with Back's expedition, published his own observations. Back was off again to the Canadian north before 1836 was out and was in print once more in 1838. The public's imagination was constantly fired by these daring attempts to push back "the boundary of ... knowledge." As the 1840s opened, there was increasing determination to find what was later described by the successful McClure as the passage that had "baffled the talented and wise for hundreds of years."[6] The wonder is not that a British potter chose the Canadian Arctic for earthenware decoration but that only one would seem to have done so.

Why the potter chose to adapt illustrations from Parry's *Journals* for the main decoration rather than any of the more current illustrations of Arctic scenery available is a question unlikely now to be answered. There was nothing unusual in turning back to illustrations of an earlier date. The economics of potting generally dictated choice. What was at hand and could be worked up with a minimum of expense must often have been the deciding factor. Josiah Wedgwood frequented the print shops of London, searching out engravings for use on pottery, but only a few British potters were ever in Wedgwood's position. A minor potter, or the pottery engraver from whom he could afford to buy a design, might have only limited opportunities for poring over the latest illustrated publications. The choice of engravings for pottery use was likely to be influenced by some chance that cannot now be fathomed.

Although it was produced in a wide choice of colours, the "Arctic Scenery" pattern is relatively rare today and so far little evidence of its sale in Canada has been found.

One family who apparently had this tableware was, appropriately, connected with fur traders from the far north. The men whose empire extended to the Arctic Sea and who, in their own way, were explorers, had a particular interest in the audacity of Arctic discoveries. In 1814 one of these traders from the Northwest returned to Lower Canada with his grandson and took up residence in Como. That grandson, Richard Story Robins, eventually married Hannah Schneider of Como, whose own family was connected with the fur trade. In the house built for Hannah in nearby Hudson Heights, on a farm that was a wedding present to her in 1836, what remained of her tablewares were preserved by her descendants. With those tablewares was earthenware with the "Arctic Scenery" pattern. How or when it was first acquired is not known.[7]

In the nineteenth century the Canadian Arctic exerted an irresistible spell over British explorers. Men who had come appallingly close to death on one expedition voluntarily set out on another. Today the search for earthenware recalling those Arctic exploits casts such a spell over collectors that almost anything depicting snow and sledges is being offered – and accepted – as a Canadian view. Collectors should be aware that scenes in Greenland or Russia can be confused with Canada. One multi-scene pattern printed on unmarked British earthenware in a blue darker than that used for "Arctic Scenery," and in date perhaps a little earlier, has been sold more than once in recent times as Canadiana. The scenes include figures and sledges taken from views not in Canada but in Siberia. They occur as illustrations in geographies published in the late eighteenth and early nineteenth centuries,[8] and probably appeared also in some travel book. To date, the only views printed on earthenware that have been documented as adapted from published illustrations of Canada's polar regions are those with the pattern name "Arctic Scenery."

CHAPTER SEVEN

Bartlett's Canadian Scenery

"... Canadian Scenery ... by W.H. Bartlett ... exquisite Engravings ..."
Royal Gazette, 21 October 1840

In the late summer of 1838 an English artist, William Henry Bartlett (Plate 32), arrived in Bytown, the settlement on the Ottawa River that was to become the capital of Canada. He had had a "tempestuous" crossing from Liverpool, but on 26 August he wrote to his friend Dr William Beattie that he had survived all the risks of the voyage and was now getting on "pretty well" with his new project. That project, which would keep him in Canada until December, was to result in *Canadian Scenery*, described by Beattie as an "elegant" production.[1] Bartlett was the illustrator, the American journalist Nathaniel P. Willis the writer of the text, George Virtue of London the publisher. That the illustrations in *Canadian Scenery* were made use of almost at once by Staffordshire potters is an indication of how popular these views of Canada were and how well they met the taste of the times.

As the *Art Union* (the London magazine later renamed the *Art Journal*) noted, Staffordshire was "obligated to cater for the public taste" and, for printed patterns on tableware, "fashion" not the manufacturers bestowed the "fiat."[2] The *Art Union*'s comment was made in 1844, at the very moment when potters were turning to these Canadian scenes for earthenware decoration.

The same nineteenth-century public ready to be awed and even moved to tears by the sublime in nature, or excited by fresh evidences of scientific progress, also wanted nature romanticized. The Victorians, whose long era was beginning at the time of Bartlett's visit to Canada, were often to favour a "softened" tone in the depiction of reality. Prince Albert, consort of Queen Victoria, spoke for his times when he commended the poet Tennyson for having blended reality "with the softer tone of the present age."[3] Taking Bartlett's Canadian views as a whole, they presented the rawness of a new country in the softer tone that the Victorians frequently preferred. Beattie was later to say of Bartlett's work that it "refines and softens," providing a "happy union" of fact and poetry.[4] Fact and poetry blended were what the Victorian age wanted, not only in books of engravings to be turned over in the drawing room (books advertised in Canada as "WORKS ... admirably suited to adorn centre tables"),[5] but as printed decoration on earthenware. At least four Staffordshire potters made use of Bartlett's Canadian scenes, all of them hurrying their tablewares onto the market shortly after the views appeared as steel engravings in Virtue's "elegant" publication.

Today Bartlett scenes are the most widely collected of all the potters' views of Canada. No collection of Canadian views on earthenware can be considered in any way representative without a good selection of them. They are neither so early nor so rare as some of the other ceramic views, but they are identified with one of the best known topographical artists of the century who depicted Canada as many Victorians desired to see it. With these views, too, the collector has the ever-alluring possibility of a new discovery.

As published in two volumes by Virtue, *Canadian Scenery* had a map and 119 views, including the frontispiece and two vignettes. In 1967 (in *Nineteenth-Century Pottery and Porcelain in Canada*), nineteen of the views were listed as having been used, either in whole or in part, on earthenware.[6] Those views (the titles given here with the variations and peculiarities of spelling as they appeared under the engravings) were:

Georgeville
Port Hope
Quebec, from the opposite shore of the St. Laurence
Kingston, – Lake Ontario
View from the Citadel at Kingston
Fish-Market, Toronto
Navy Island (from the Canada side)
Hallowell (Bay of Quintè)
Village of Cedars, River St. Lawrence
Montreal (from the St. Lawrence)
The Chaudière Bridge (near Quebec)
The Rideau Canal, Bytown
Church at Point-Levi
Outlet of Lake Memphremagog
The Governor's House, Fredericton
Indian Scene
St. John and Portland, New Brunswick
Lily Lake (St. John)
View of the City of Halifax, Nova Scotia. From Dartmouth

Since 1967 at least eight more Bartlett views, or parts of them, have been added to the list (again, the titles are as they appeared under the engravings):

Fort Chambly
St. Regis, Indian Village (St. Lawrence)
Lake of the two Mountains
Scene among the Thousand Isles
Brockville, – St. Laurence
The Green at Fredericton
A Shanty on Lake Chaudière (Canada)
Windsor, Nova Scotia. From the residence of Judge Haliburton, author of "Sam
   Slick"

The potters' interest in these pictures of Indians and birch-bark canoes, of timber rafts on the mighty St Lawrence, and settlements emerging from primeval forest, of garrison towns and New World harbours filled with tall-masted ships was promoted, as the *Art Union* said, by the public's interest. The public's interest was due to two things: the Victorian fascination with faraway lands and romantic places (for so Canada seemed to many in the Old World) and Bartlett's own reputation.

Born in 1809, William Henry Bartlett was still in his twenties when he came to Canada in the summer of 1838, but already he was the well-known illustrator of nearly a dozen works. By the time of his death in 1854, the list had grown to almost thirty volumes. As early as 1840, when his Canadian scenes began appearing "in parts," he was described as the illustrator of works "widely circulated abroad," and at home in England "seen on every table" (meaning, in this context, on drawing room and parlour tables).[7] Their popularity lasted. In 1861 Henry Shaw, a Montreal auctioneer, was offering Virtue's "BEAUTIFULLY BOUND AND ILLUSTRATED ... BOOKS" in a "SPLENDID CHRISTMAS ... SALE."[8] The list included nine works with illustrations by Bartlett. The *Art Journal's* obituary credited Bartlett with having helped to raise topographical art to a new artistic status. He himself believed that "the study of topography" had the power to make "every country ... an object ... of interest."[9] It made Canada an object of interest not only to the buyers of what today would be called coffee table books but to buyers of earthenware for the dinner table.

Willis's text for *Canadian Scenery* was scarcely equal to Bartlett's illustrations. It was largely a scissors-and-paste effort, relying heavily on quotations from other writers, some of whose impressions of Canada related to an earlier period and were hardly relevant in the early Victorian years. The two men, the American Willis and the Englishman Bartlett, could not have been more different. Willis, whom S.C. Hall, the editor of the *Art Journal*, remembered as too much of the dandy,[10] was satirized by his sister in the United States as "a toady and a cad."[11] While allowances might be made for the peculiar bitterness of family feuds, the truth was that Willis actively cultivated the titled and rich, making his way by set purpose when abroad into glittering social circles. By contrast, Bartlett was unconquerably shy, indifferent to dress, and totally lacking the essential pushiness of the social climber. More important, his was a life of what Dr Beattie, his biographer, called "unremitting industry."[12] He relied on none but himself for his pictorial information. He travelled, often at worrisome expense and under hardship, to every country he was commissioned to illustrate. Pirates, robbers, cholera, the chance of shipwreck (as on his voyage to Canada in 1838) were all part of the hazards of his work.

In his efforts to provide for his family, Bartlett lived "the life of an exile." He described himself as "a machine, destined to perform ... a certain *quantum* of work ... then break down and be thrown aside."[13] In this he was prophetic: his work killed him. On the way home from an exhausting trip to Asia Minor, Bartlett fell ill at sea. Worn out, he died on the evening of 13 September 1854. The next morning the British passengers and the ship's officers aboard the French ship, *Egyptus*, gathered in a little group on deck. The burial service was read in English. Bartlett's remains, encased "in a hasty shroud," were "slowly raised by the hands of strangers – then lowered – and consigned to their ocean grave."[14] The man whose views are the best known of all Canadian scenes, to china and print collector alike, was only forty-five at the time of his death. His dream of providing independence for his family – a dream that was always receding into the distance – was gone forever.

Canadian Scenery came a little before the mid-point in Bartlett's career. The work in Canada was completed by the end of 1838.[15] Two years later Virtue was able to announce publication. A New Brunswick advertisement of 21 October that year gave details of its appearance in monthly parts:

> *Published under the Patronage of ... the Queen.* Canadian Scenery Illustrated FROM original Drawings by W.H. Bartlett, whose labors have already illustrated Scotland, Switzerland ... Palestine, &c. &c ... the Historical and descriptive parts by N.P. Willis, Esquire.
> A part will be published regularly every month; each part will contain four exquisite Engravings ... price 3s. 9d. each part ...[16]

According to Beattie, Virtue brought out *Canadian Scenery* in book form in 1842.[17] It was published originally in two volumes, but those who had subscribed to the "parts" and then had them bound could, naturally, have them bound in any way they wished.

W. Dunbar, who advertised in 1840 that he was "the sole Agent" for *Canadian Scenery* in New Brunswick and Nova Scotia, also advertised *American Scenery*, another Virtue publication with text by Willis and illustrations by Bartlett. Bartlett's visit to Canada in 1838 was his second to North America; he had previously spent twelve months, in 1836 and 1837, in the United States, working on the sketches for *American Scenery*. The linking of *Canadian Scenery* and *American Scenery* in the New Brunswick advertisement had its counterpart in the work of a Staffordshire potter, Thomas Godwin of Burslem. In the 1840s Godwin produced a multi-scene pattern in which he made extensive use of *American Scenery*, but his pattern also included at least two subjects adapted from *Canadian Scenery*: "Outlet of Lake Memphremagog," used on the covers of gravy tureens, and "Village of Cedars," used on small plates (Plate 33).

The maker's mark on Godwin's wares included the Royal Arms, the potter's name and address (T. GODWIN, WHARF), the pattern name (AMERICAN VIEWS), the type of

FIGURE 10
P.W. & Co. marks

earthenware body (OPAQUE CHINA), and the title of the Bartlett view on that particular piece (on the plates, for example, "Village of Cedars"). The floral border featured nasturtiums and convolvulus. The pattern was offered in blue, brown, or in varying shades of pink.

The date of introduction of this pattern is obviously determined not by the main source of the decoration (*American Scenery*) but by *Canadian Scenery*, just slightly later in date. From the appearance of the wares, the pattern is unlikely to have been introduced much before 1845; it may have been later (Godwin was in business until 1854).

By choosing the pattern name "American Views," Godwin not only acknowledged the main source of the decoration but also made clear that the United States market was uppermost in his mind. It is interesting to note, however, that he must have been aware of the possibilities for business in Canada. His connection with another Staffordshire potter, Benjamin Godwin, would have ensured it. Benjamin, with whom Thomas had formerly been in partnership and to whom he was presumably related, was an active exporter to Canada. The evidence lies in wares made by him in the 1830s, which carry the name of a Montreal importer of those days, John Glennon.[18]

Thomas Godwin called his pattern "American Views" and aimed for the American market. Another Staffordshire firm, Podmore, Walker & Co., also active in the 1840s and 1850s, brought out a multi-scene pattern based on Bartlett's Canadian scenes and named it "British America" (Figure 10). Their prime target for sales were the colonies in British America. Thomas Podmore, Thomas Walker, and Enoch Wedgwood (the "& Co." in the firm's name)[19] had built up a strong Canadian connection; it would have been the solid assurance of an established trade that justified the expense of a pattern intended primarily for Canadian sale (British America as opposed to the United States). Wares such as tea bowls inexpensively painted in "peasant style," printed wares with romanticized scenes of lands that never were, and small plates meant to amuse and instruct children all laid the foundations of Podmore, Walker & Co.'s success in Canada, and made it feasible to launch a new pattern which involved the engraving of many new copperplates. The National Museum of Man has examples of all the types of wares with which this enterprising firm won sales in British America, including a child's plate with a history of use in Newfoundland.[20]

The "British America" pattern was almost certainly in production in the 1840s. An unexpected and important clue to the date when it first came on the market was found buried in a Halifax newspaper advertisement.[21] In 1843 in the *Novascotian*, an importer named John McDonald announced fresh supplies of china and earthenware just in from England. Among these latest goods were "Patterns" for "Dinner Sets" of printed earthenware "with British North American Views" (Plate 34). The advertisement ran for two years.

The words "British North American Views" at once suggest Podmore, Walker & Co.'s pattern name "British America." The year 1843 links earthenware with Canadian views to a date when *Canadian Scenery*, advertised in parts in 1840 and published in book form in 1842, would have been available to Staffordshire potters. No other pottery firm and no other views of Canada appear to provide the answer to what John McDonald of Halifax was advertising at the end of 1843.

One of the great attractions Podmore, Walker & Co.'s "British America" holds for Canadian collectors is that it was a pattern intended for sale in the British North American colonies. It would be a mistake, however, to think of it as a pattern whose original sale was solely to Canadians. Few of the potters' views of Canada were restricted to any one market. In recent years sufficient evidence has come to light to show there was a sale of this pattern in Great Britain itself. In Canada, its sale was not in any way limited to the Atlantic area. Families in the Eastern Townships of Quebec had "British America" table services which their descendants have inherited. Even the bottom of the upper St Lawrence River has yielded up shards, at a point where forwarders from Montreal used to pass with their cargoes on the way to Kingston. Dr R.P. Harpur of McGill University was scuba diving at Windmill Point, near Prescott, Ontario, on the afternoon of 19 August 1973 when he spotted a fragment of broken crockery on the river-bed. He picked up what proved to be the major part of a blue-printed "British America" plate. Later that same afternoon his diving partner, Kenneth Hugessen of Montreal, laid on the shore another fragment of crockery he had retrieved farther along the stony river bottom. Someone else in the diving party noticed that the two shards seemed to belong together. When cleaned and joined, the shards made up a plate with only one small piece missing. The view on it was Navy Island.[22]

Podmore, Walker & Co. made more extensive use of *Canadian Scenery* than any other Staffordshire firm. To date, the list of views they adapted in whole or in part has reached twenty, and includes such cities or towns as Halifax, Windsor, Saint John, Fredericton (two), Quebec (Plates 35, 36), Montreal (Plates 37, 38), Brockville, Port

FIGURE 11
P.W. & Co. mark

Hope (Plate 39), Kingston (two) (Plates 40, 41, 42), and Toronto. They also made use of Navy Island (the view retrieved from the bottom of the St Lawrence), the Chaudière Bridge (Plates 43, 47), Lily Lake, St Regis (Indian Village), Indian scene on the St Lawrence (Plates 45, 46), Village of Cedars (the same view used by Thomas Godwin), Lake of Two Mountains, and Fort Chambly. It is entirely within the realm of possibility that still other views may come to light and that articles not yet recorded in this pattern will be found.

All the usual articles of dinner, breakfast, tea, and toilet wares were made. There are, for example, ewers and basins with a view of Quebec; covered vegetable dishes with views of the Governor's House at Fredericton (Plates 47, 48, 49), or the view of Windsor, Nova Scotia; sauce tureens with the Chaudière Bridge; meat dishes of all sizes with Montreal or Halifax on the largest, Brockville on the smallest; plates for soup, dinner, or pudding with Lily Lake, a scene in the Thousand Isles, Kingston, or Navy Island; there are even the small plates that North American collectors usually call cup plates, but whose use was probably more varied, decorated with a detail from the view Bartlett entitled "St Regis, Indian Village" (Plates 50, 51).

The body used for the "British America" pattern, as well as for most of the other tablewares exported to Canada by Podmore, Walker & Co., was marked PEARL STONE WARE (impressed). The "British America" wares usually (but not always) had in addition an ornate printed mark combining the Royal Arms, the name of the pattern, the maker's initials, and the title of the Bartlett view appearing on the piece (Figure 11). In the case of tureens with stands and covered vegetable dishes, only the stand or the dish (not the cover) might be marked. An exception is the large vegetable dish with a view of the Lake of Two Mountains on the cover and Windsor on the inside of the dish itself. Both views are identified, the title "Lake OF THE TWO MOUNTAINS" appearing within a cartouche on the inside of the cover, the full printed mark being on the bottom of the dish.

The same scene did not always appear on the same article. For example, Brockville is found on open vegetable dishes and on small meat dishes. Some views were used as main decoration and also as additional decoration around the sides of a dish or on a cover. The Chaudière Bridge was the main decoration on sauce tureens; it was also used on the sides of vegetable dishes and on some covers.

The border on Podmore, Walker & Co.'s "British America" does not appear in full on every piece, but when it does it is a graceful one of flower heads and fern-like fronds above a vermicular design, finished off by a narrow line of foliage.

Podmore, Walker & Co. produced their "British America" in several colours: light blue, sepia, a reddish brown, or black. Occasionally it is found in a light green and it also turns up in a slightly darker blue. How long the pattern remained in production is impossible to say, but it was available for some years. The long-running advertisement in the *Novascotian*, the range of colours, and the fact that hollow wares are found in more than one shape (octagonal and lobed) suggest a not inconsiderable life span. The firm itself was in business until the end of the 1850s.

Working from *Canadian Scenery*, the pottery's engraver had over a hundred views from which to make a choice. He dwelt heavily on the tranquil. Timber rafts drift peacefully down New World rivers, a colonial governor's house nestles into luxuriant greenery, Highlanders from the garrison at Kingston take their ease by Lake Ontario. As was always the case when published views were taken over for ceramic decoration, changes were made. In "British America" these changes frequently accented the picturesque. There was not a canoe to be seen in Bartlett's view of the Chaudière Bridge, but on Podmore, Walker & Co.'s tableware two birch-bark canoes, with their great curved ends, are conspicuous in the foreground, the bridge looming in the distance behind them (Plate 43). Again, one of the more picturesque touches of the Canadian scene in those nineteenth-century days was the presence of soldiers from the garrisons. Bartlett used them in a number of his views but did not introduce them into his view of Quebec, taken from the opposite shore. The pottery engraver added them, placing a soldier with his wife and child in the foreground, their presence not only picturesque but lending a quiet, domestic touch (Plate 36). Nothing in these potters' views of Canada disturbs: British America is seen with romantic serenity.

CHAPTER EIGHT

Morley's Bartlett Views

"Mr. Morley ... entered with spirit into the ... business."
Llewellynn Jewitt, 1878

The potter whose Bartlett views of Canada were in production over the longest period was Francis Morley. Morley came on the market with an even wider range of colours than Podmore, Walker & Co., offered his Canadian scenes at two price levels (with or without added gilding), registered one of the shapes on which the Canadian views appeared, and produced a pattern his successors found worthwhile to bring back in the 1880s.

Morley began potting on his own account in 1845,[1] but his connection with the British North American colonies began well before that date. He was a son-in-law of William Ridgway, a member of one of Staffordshire's chief potting families and a manufacturer who had visited Canada to assess the market for himself.[2] Ridgway, who had a chain of agents in North America, became so immersed in the export trade that at one time he contemplated setting up a pottery in the United States. In Staffordshire he owned a number of potbanks and worked in various partnerships. Two of the partnerships involved his son-in-law.

William Ridgway, his son-in-law Francis Morley, and a third partner named William Wear (chief bailiff of Shelton and Hanley in 1839) were in business as Ridgway, Morley, Wear & Co. from 1835 to 1842.[3] They were probably the first to use the illustrations by William Henry Bartlett that appeared in *Canadian Scenery*. Their use of Canadian views, however, was only incidental. Under the name "Agricultural Vase," the firm brought out a multi-scene pattern in which a variety of landscapes provided the background to an impressive covered urn decorated with symbols of agriculture and surmounted by a figure of Ceres (in mythology, the personification of the harvest and protectress of agriculture). The vase was sometimes on the right, sometimes on the left, but always the dominant feature of the design.

One of the backgrounds was a composite scene made up of elements from three or four Bartlett views of Canada. "The Outlet of Lake Memphremagog" (Plate 52) provided the main part, but the pottery engraver made changes at both ends of the bridge in this view. At one end he inserted a cabin taken from "A Shanty on Lake Chaudière"; at the other, a haywagon borrowed from "Quebec from the opposite shore of the St. Laurence." He also introduced a steamboat. In Bartlett's "Outlet of Lake Memphremagog" an indistinct boat in the far distance is nothing more than a blur, its lines too indefinite for identification. On earthenware the boat moved into the middle distance as a two-funnelled side-wheeler. Boats of this type are in half a dozen or more of Bartlett's Canadian scenes. Possibly the pottery engraver was inspired by a steamboat in the same view from which he took the haywagon.

Printed in light blue, pink, purple, brown, or green, the pattern was used on dinner ware, the Canadian composite scene occurring on both plates and hollow pieces. The collections of the National Museum of Man include, among other examples of this pattern, a large covered vegetable dish (Plate 53). On the cover is an unidentified view; the Canadian scene appears on the interior of the dish, which is octagonal (Plate 54). The border for this pattern, composed of moss-like sprays and four-petalled flowers, bears some resemblance to the border known as Catskill Moss, which William Ridgway, in another of his partnerships, used in the early 1840s to surround views adapted from *American Scenery* and intended for sale in the United States.[4]

The marks on the "Agricultural Vase" pattern vary. Usually there is an ornate, printed mark with another two-handled vase, the pattern name, the words IMPROVED GRANITE CHINA, and the initials RMW & CO. (Figure 12). The printed mark is often accompanied by an impressed one in which the words GRANITE CHINA appear on a shield (a mark also found on other wares made by William Ridgway when potting under his own name alone).

The pattern was first introduced towards the close of Ridgway, Morley, Wear & Co.'s partnership. The use made of *Canadian Scenery* establishes this. In book form, *Canadian Scenery* came out in 1842 (the year Ridgway, Morley & Co.'s partnership ended). Even if the pottery engraver had worked from the monthly "parts" of *Canadian Scenery*, for which booksellers were taking orders in the autumn of 1840,[5] the pattern could scarcely have been on the market before 1841. But the end of Ridgway, Morley, Wear & Co. was not the end of the "Agricultural Vase." The pattern was carried on during the second partnership Ridgway formed with Morley. As Ridgway & Morley, the two potted together from 1842 to 1844.[6] Tablewares printed with the "Agricultural Vase" may be found with the makers' initials R & M.

In 1845 Morley began business on his own account, first trading as Francis Morley and then, from 1850 to 1858, as Francis Morley & Co. (his partner during this period was Samuel Astbury).[7] Examples of the "Agricultural Vase" pattern carrying both the old, ornate printed mark with the outdated makers' initials, RMW & CO., together with the impressed mark of F. MORLEY & CO., indicate the pattern was in production at least as late as 1850 (the year "& Co." became part of Morley's business style).

In the history of potters' views of Canada, the "Agricultural Vase," with its scraps of Canadian scenery, is of only minor importance, but the connection with Francis

FIGURE 12
R.M.W. & Co. mark

Morley is significant, for Morley, branching out on his own, was to make the scenery of Canada known to a far wider public than any other potter.

Marriage, not birth, brought Morley into the world of potting. Contrary to what might be expected, he was not a Staffordshire man. He was a native of Nottingham, the son of a successful hosiery manufacturer. He was, however, to prove a most suitable in-law for the Ridgways, whose potting antecedents went back to the eighteenth century. Energetic, astute, and, like his father-in-law, a supporter of Methodism (a strong influence in the Potteries), Morley threw himself into potting. Llewellynn Jewitt, the nineteenth-century historian, summed up Morley's career when he said that he entered "with spirit" into the pottery business and into the life of Staffordshire.[8] His marriage to Emma Ridgway took place in the autumn of 1835. Less than four years later he was actively engaged, with Charles James Mason (the celebrated patentee of Ironstone China), in seeking improved railway communications for the district.[9] Once the promoters of canals to facilitate getting their wares to ports such as Liverpool, the Staffordshire potters of early Victorian days were increasingly aware of the advantages of rail communications. One evidence of Morley's business perception was his quick grasp of all that would promote an export trade.

Morley's business connections with his father-in-law had brought him into contact with the North American market, and had also, in the "Agricultural Vase" pattern, introduced him to *Canadian Scenery*. As soon as he began potting on his own he capitalized on what he had learned. Podmore, Walker & Co. were already offering the public a pattern that made extensive use of Bartlett's Canadian views, but their "British America" pattern, by virtue of its name alone, had greater appeal in Canada than in the

United States. Morley was quick to sense the profits to be gained by exploiting both markets equally with one pattern. He achieved that end with a multi-scene pattern that featured Bartlett's popular views of Canada but whose name had no nationalistic connotations. "Lake" was the vague and generalized name chosen by Morley. His multi-scene pattern drew upon at least ten different Bartlett views. Almost half of them had already been used by Podmore, Walker & Co.; all of them had the attractions of picturesque and romanticized scenery that appealed equally in Quebec or New York, Halifax or Philadelphia.

Water was in each of the views, although "lake" was scarcely an apt description for the tidal waters lapping under the heights of Quebec (as seen from Levis), or the man-diverted water in the canal at Bytown. None the less, in taking "Lake" as his pattern name, Morley chose a title that had its own allure at the time. In early Victorian days the most popular of all the imaginary, or fanciful, pictorial designs – and there were many more of these than designs based on actual topographical views – were those featuring a lake of some sort. Literally scores of imaginary lake scenes were turned out by potters in Staffordshire, Tyneside, Scotland, and Wales, all competing for what a commentator of the day called the potter's "great prize": the public's financially rewarding approval.[10] General storekeepers as far from Staffordshire as Yarmouth, Nova Scotia, believed that a lake scene had sales appeal. An advertisement inserted in the *Yarmouth Herald* by Joseph and John Tooker on 2 January 1841 promised customers tableware patterns that would include "lakes." At that date, the Yarmouth advertisement would not have been referring to Morley's "Lake"; it was simply a reference to a type of pictorial decoration on earthenware that colonial importers were confident would attract buyers. Morley's choice of pattern name reflected both his own perceptive business sense and the taste of the times.

Morley introduced his "Lake" pattern very soon after he began potting under his own name. The clue to the date is in the marks on a tureen acquired a few years ago by the National Museum of Man (Plate 55). The marks include not only the printed pattern name but also the impressed diamond-shaped registry mark and, encircling it and also impressed, the words: REGISTERED BY F. MORLEY 31st MAY 1845 (Figure 13). The registration at the British Patent Office (design number 27800) was not for the pattern itself but for what the application described as "dinner service" shapes. The relevant page in the Register of Designs shows a drawing of a soup tureen (the same shape as the museum's tureen) and a covered vegetable dish (Plate 56). Morley was, therefore, using his "Lake" pattern on a shape registered in the year he began business.

Registration of either a pattern or shape was usually for a period of three years. During this time the manufacturer had copyright protection. He could renew the registration, but Morley did not do so. The combination of the diamond-shaped registry mark, which gives in code the date and holder of the registration, and that same information emphasized in the impressed Morley name and date suggest that the museum's tureen was produced when the registration of its shape was new or, in any event, within the period 1845–8. If this is the case, then the "Lake" pattern, printed on the tureen, can be dated close to 1845. The fact that Podmore, Walker & Co. had a

FIGURE 13
Registration mark (Morley)

pattern based on *Canadian Scenery* in production in the mid-1840s is a corroborating reason for setting a date of about 1845 for the introduction of Morley's pattern. There was keen competition among the potters and both firms were active in the North American export trade.

The same registration date of 31 May 1845 has also been found on covered vegetable dishes and on sauce boats and their stands in the "Lake" pattern. Articles noted with the date mark are normally those with the distinctive handles shown in the drawings accompanying the application for registration of shape (Plates 57, 58). Some plates had rims moulded with a running leaf design, the leaves being somewhat similar to the moulded leaves on the covers of tureens and vegetable dishes, but the plates, like most "Lake" articles, seem to have been marked with the printed pattern name only.

Morley's pattern name, "LAKE," appears in an ornamental device adapted from the central span of the Chaudière Bridge (Figure 14), a Bartlett view used on both soup and dinner plates, as well as on the covers and sides of some dishes (Plates 59, 60). Unlike Podmore, Walker & Co., Morley made no attempt to identify the Bartlett engravings used.

The views Morley shared with Podmore, Walker & Co. were those of the Chaudière Bridge, a view of Kingston (Plate 61), the Indian scene on the St Lawrence (Plate 62), and the Village of Cedars (Plate 63). Bartlett's work inspired both Morley's "Lake" and Podmore, Walker & Co.'s "British America," but each firm made its own adaptations. In the Village of Cedars, for instance, Morley omitted the wayside cross seen at the left of the view in *Canadian Scenery*; Podmore, Walker & Co. retained it (Plates 64, 65, 66).

FIGURE 14
Morley's "Lake" mark

In addition to the views shared with Podmore, Walker & Co., Morley also adapted:

Outlet of Lake Memphremagog (Plate 67)
The Rideau Canal, Bytown (Plates 68, 69)
Hallowell (Bay of Quintè) (Plate 70)
Scene among the Thousand Isles (Plates 71, 72, 73)
Georgeville (Plate 74)
Church at Point-Levi (Plate 75)

The "Lake" pattern included, too, a typical European lake scene that had nothing at all to do with *Canadian Scenery* (the source for all the other views in the series). With its mountain-girt lake and European-style castle in the distance, it was typical of the idealized view that had endless appeal at the time (Plates 76, 77). It was the sort of view the Tookers were offering Nova Scotia buyers in 1841. Injecting an unrelated scene into a multi-scene pattern was not so unusual as it might seem. Morley had good precedents for it. In Regency days Josiah Spode had done the same thing, when he produced a pattern based on published views of Asia Minor and included one curiously composite scene with non-Asiatic elements.[11]

The border for the "Lake" pattern (Plate 78) was composed of garlands of flowers and scrolls (or stylized foliage). The effect was heavier than Podmore, Walker & Co.'s border.

Morley's pattern turns up in an unexpectedly wide range of colours: light blue, a darker blue, mauve, grey, green, brown, pink, and a clear, bright purple. All of these colours have been recorded in public or private collections, but what many collectors do not know is that Morley also offered this pattern with added gilding on hollow pieces in the registered shape. Good quality gold was used to outline the moulded leaves and to pick out details in the realistic twig handles. Covers for tureens and vegetable dishes had a pronounced loop and dot design painted in gold between the view and the border, the border itself being outlined in gold. Table services with added gilding would have been more expensive than those with underglaze printed decoration only. The "Lake" pattern was used by Morley on more than one shape, but gilding has been noted only on the shape that was registered.

The variety of articles found in this pattern is astonishing. In addition to all the usual items of tea, dinner, and toilet wares (including foot baths), there are covered custard cups, cheese stands, children's mugs, toy table services, ladles for tureens of all sizes, egg cups and the stands to hold them. There are also jugs with dragon handles, reminiscent in shape of some of Charles James Mason's jugs. Morley purchased copper-plates and moulds from Mason when that brilliant, volatile potter stumbled into bankruptcy in 1848, which may explain the shape of the Morley jugs.[12]

Among the rarest items in the "Lake" pattern are large, ornamental vases. The National Museum of Man has two pairs, one covered (frontispiece, Plate 79). Each is printed in green with the "Outlet of Lake Memphremagog" (Plate 52). The Georgeville scene is on the covers. The two pairs, which appear to be of the same date and which were acquired from the same source, may have been intended as a garniture.

Although Morley did not take as many views from *Canadian Scenery* as did Podmore, Walker & Co., he made maximum use of those he selected. The Georgeville scene decorates not only the covers of vases but tea bowls and their saucers, teapots, small plates, the outside of footed salad bowls, and the stands for gravy tureens (Plate 80). The Indian scene appears on cream jugs, plates, and on the covers of dishes and tureens. A part of it was used on the bowls of small ladles.

That Morley successfully achieved his goal of producing Canadian views that would appeal to American as well as Canadian buyers is proved by the existence of wares carrying the names of American importers.[13] While no Canadian importers' names have so far been recorded on any example of the "Lake" pattern, there is ample evidence that Canadian families owned it. An eminent Canadian who had it on his dinner table was Sir William Dawson, the Novascotian educator and scientist who became principal of McGill University shortly after mid-century. Sir William, who achieved the distinction of becoming president of both the British Association for the Advancement of Science and the American Association, took pride in the fact that he was a British American. Bartlett's Canadian views on tableware would have made a direct appeal to him. His service was in the shape registered in 1845 and may have been purchased at the time of his marriage in 1847. It formed part of the household possessions the Dawsons shipped to Montreal by the *Lady Head*, when Sir William left Nova Scotia for McGill in 1855.[14] The collections of the National Museum of Man have two pieces from the Dawson service, the gift of Mrs Lois Winslow-Spragge, a grand-daughter of Sir William and Lady Dawson.

One of the rare gilded services was acquired by the Ewing family of Montreal. The Ewings emigrated from Scotland in the nineteenth century and eventually established a large-scale seed business in the Province of Quebec. Until recently, what remained of this service was in the possession of a descendant. It is now distributed between public and private collections.

Another table service, with a family tradition of having been purchased in Scotland and sent out to Canada, has been handed down in a Maritime family. No documentation supports the family tradition, but there is no doubt Morley's Canadian views had a sale in Great Britain. The amount of the "Lake" pattern found there in recent years by Canadians searching for it bears this out. It was in England that one Canadian, some years ago, discovered an almost complete toy service (printed in grey with details taken from the Indian scene on the St Lawrence and the view of the Village of Cedars). Others have come upon plates, tea bowls, and dishes in country antique shops, not only in England but in Ireland and Scotland. Significantly, the important documentary soup tureen belonging to the National Museum of Man was found in Great Britain.

The "Lake" pattern had a long life. The occasional example marked F.M. & CO. (usually seen on wares which also have the name of the Philadelphia importers Tyndale & Mitchell) shows that Morley was still making it after he formed his partnership with Samuel Astbury in 1850. In 1858 that partnership was dissolved, and from then until 1862, when Morley retired, he was in partnership with Taylor Ashworth. In 1862 the firm became George L. Ashworth & Brothers. The Ashworth interest was bought out in 1883 by John Hackett Goddard, but the business style of George L. Ashworth & Brothers was retained.[15]

It is possible that Morley and Ashworth continued the "Lake" pattern during their brief partnership: marked specimens would prove it (the mark would be MORLEY & ASHWORTH or the initials M & A). It is not surprising that Morley kept in production for some time a successful pattern. What is surprising is that his successors found it worth while to revive it in the 1880s, printing it from copperplates newly engraved in a coarser style. These Ashworth wares carry the old "Lake" mark, the name ASHWORTH impressed, and often a date code for February 1884. The printing is usually on a rather heavy earthenware of a cream or ivory colour. (In the 1880s "ivory" was a term for what in earlier times would have been described simply as "cream.")[16] When Morley introduced the pattern in the 1840s the printing had been against a white background, the glaze on the earthenware sometimes slightly blued to make the appearance of the body whiter still.

How long the "Lake" pattern remained in production is uncertain. There are some wares in it and some marks difficult to date precisely. Wares, for example, with the pattern name only (no maker's mark) and impressed BEST GOODS probably date after the end of the 1850s but within the nineteenth century. Some wares with the pattern name only and coarsely printed in a very blurred, deep blue almost certainly belong to the twentieth century. The question is how late in the twentieth century. In the 1960s the Ashworth firm still had some of the old copperplates for the "Lake" pattern, although no one could recall their having been used for half a century or more.[17] Of greatest interest to collectors, however, will be those examples of the pattern made during Morley's own period.

There were many potters' views of Canada in the nineteenth century, but only one potter, Francis Morley, keen man of affairs and builder of "a lucrative business,"[18] was able to give Canadian scenery so long a life on the dinner tables of two continents.

CHAPTER NINE

Maple Leaves and Beavers

"Canada ... has two emblems ... the *Beaver* and the *Maple*."
Sir William Dawson, 27 November 1863

The potters' conception of Canada included more than topographical views: an aware-ness of Canadian emblems provided two Staffordshire potters with designs for table and toilet ware decoration. These wares differed from the topographical views in one important aspect. The topographical views, with rare exceptions, made a general appeal to the nineteenth-century interest in geography and the romance of distant lands. Their sales potential was not necessarily restricted. By contrast, wares with maple leaves and beavers made a patriotic appeal in Canada but were without significance in other parts of the world.

The earlier of these Staffordshire wares had an appeal that was restricted even within the British North American colonies themselves. Shortly after mid-century Edward Walley of Cobridge produced earthenware decorated with maple leaves and beavers (Plate 83) and, in addition, with mottoes significant only in what was then Canada East (now the Province of Quebec). One motto was in French, one in Latin: NOS INSTITUTIONS! NOTRE LANGUE, ET NOS LOIS, and LABOR OMNIA VINCIT. The origin of the wares may have been in a special order, but the wares were not a special order in the usual narrow sense. Their sale was not confined to a particular family or institution (as were wares ordered with a monogram or the name or initials of a hotel, hospital, or company). These were wares with a broad appeal to French Canadians and, within the limits of that appeal, their original sale was general. They have been handed down in old families in Quebec and have been discovered forgotten in cupboards in convents and other Roman Catholic institutions.

Just when maple leaves and beavers first became acknowledged Canadian symbols is debatable. A French-Canadian writer of the 1890s, dealing with this same question, pointed out that such things seem to develop of their own accord: "il est bien difficile de préciser l'origine des coutumes et des usages populaires ... ces chose-là naissent on ne sait où, ni comment, ni pourquoi."[1]

From the earliest days of settlement the maple tree had played a prominent role in the lives of the colonists. Gédéon de Catalogne, a French engineer who came to Canada in 1683 and who had charge of erecting fortifications for the defence of Quebec and Louisbourg, reported on its importance in a letter written from Quebec in 1712 to the government in France. The maple, he said, had the merit of being found in abundance everywhere, was suitable for furniture-making, provided excellent heat in winter, and in the spring was the source of what he called the "eau sucrée."[2] By the next century the maple leaf had become an accepted emblem of French Canada. In a speech delivered in Montreal on 24 June 1836, Denis Benjamin Viger, a nationalist leader, called it "L'embleme du peuple canadien."[3]

The pelt of the beaver had been the staple of the fur trade from the beginning of the French régime. The same year that Viger, president of the Montreal St Jean Baptiste Society, described the maple leaf as the emblem of French Canadians, the *Canadien*, a nationalist newspaper published in Quebec City, dropped its front page "vignette" of a habitant with his plough and oxen and replaced it with maple leaves and a beaver. This "frontispice," said the *Canadien*, needed no explanation: "les emblems ... sont tous faciles à comprendre."[4]

The slogan "nos institutions! notre langue, et nos lois" has been attributed to two sources. Etienne Parent, editor of the *Canadien* in the 1820s and again in the 1830s (when the paper, suppressed in 1825, was revived), used it on the front page. Joseph François Perrault, generally regarded as "the father of education in French Canada," used it as the title of a pamphlet published in 1832. No matter who used it first, both men helped to popularize it. When it was adopted in 1844 as the motto of the recently formed Quebec City branch of the St Jean Baptiste Society, its general usage among nationalists spread even further. Other branches of the society took it up, and on every twenty-fourth of June (the saint's feast day) it was prominently displayed. So identified with French-Canadian sentiment did it become that Victorian visitors to Canada commented upon it. " 'Nos institutions, notre langue, nos lois' is the motto of the *habitants*," wrote Sir Charles Wentworth Dilke, the English author and politician, in a travel book published in 1868.[5]

The motto "labor omnia vincit" was allied with both education and nationalism in Quebec. It was the official motto of the Department of Public Instruction of Lower Canada. Combined with religious symbols, maple leaves, and a beaver, it appeared on printed forms of the department and on book labels, such as those put into school prizes. In 1857 it was adopted as the logo of the *Journal de l'instruction*, a government-sponsored teachers' periodical that "blended nationalism, religion, work, and science."[6]

These are the sources of the emblems and mottoes on Walley's heavy ironstone china. Any wares decorated with them would have made a strong appeal to the whole spectrum of French-Canadian nationalist sentiment. Such wares, in a tough, durable body, were suitable for the crockery needs of religious and educational institutions or

FIGURE 15
Registration mark (Walley)

organizations such as the St Jean Baptiste Society, and for use in any French-Canadian homes where practicality and sentiment were requisites for tablewares (Plate 81).

Who placed the order with Walley has yet to be ascertained, but it is possible that some enterprising Canadian china merchant had a role in the project. E.Z. Massicotte, the archivist and historian, believed this was the case and that the china merchant was Henry Howison of Quebec City.[7] Whether or not Howison did actually expedite the order, Quebec directories show he was active in the earthenware importing trade at the time these wares must have been made.

The approximate date of the wares can be determined by the fact the printed decoration was used on teapots, jugs, tureens, etc., whose shape was registered at the Patent Office in London on 29 November 1856 (Plate 82). The shape was called "Niagara," and this name, together with Walley's name and the date of registration, was impressed on the bottom of most pieces (Figure 15). Modern reference books for British ceramic marks give Walley's working period as 1845–56. But, on the basis of the Canadian evidence alone, it was impossible to think that 1856 could be the cut-off date for Walley. The amount of the ware in the "Niagara" shape found in Canada – not only the ware with French-Canadian symbols, but wares in this same shape with painted decoration, sponged decoration, or no decoration at all – made it absurd to think it could all have been produced in the last month of 1856 (or after 29 November, when the registration of the shape and the right to use that date in the mark became official). Llewellynn Jewitt gave 1865 as the closing date for Walley's pottery (in both the 1878 and 1883 editions of his *Ceramic Art of Great Britain*) and this, in fact, is the correct date for the cessation of Walley's business. The corroborating information is in records preserved at the City Museum and Art Galley in Stoke-on-Trent, Staffordshire, and which have been consulted and the information made available by the Museum's director, Arnold Mountford.

In the wares for the French-Canadian market the underglaze transfer printing was in grey. Occasionally the grey was almost a light blue. There was a choice of borders. Some table services and toilet sets had a printed floral border, others simply a gold line around the rim. There were services with blue and red enamel bands (Plate 84), and services with a combination of enamel colour and gilding for a border. What were probably the cheapest had no border decoration at all, printed or painted. A notable feature of these wares is the generous size of dinner and soup plates. Teaware, too, is usually larger than the normal wares of mid-century date (Plate 85).

On some of Walley's meat dishes the words PARIS WHITE are impressed. There was no connection with Paris: "Paris White" was merely another of Staffordshire's methods of forcing a heavy earthenware body into effective competition with inexpensive French porcelain. In the second half of the nineteenth century British earthenware of the ironstone type was often given a slightly grey-white look (what Walley was calling "Paris White") that resulted in a superficial resemblance to the cheaper kinds of French porcelain. Cheap French porcelain had begun to make inroads into markets once almost entirely served by the earthenware potters. The earthenware potters had their own methods of combating competition, and names such as "French China" (an impressed mark used by another Staffordshire potter, Charles Meigh) or "Porcelaine Opaque" (used by Sampson Bridgwood & Son) cast an aura of porcelain gentility over wares that were not porcelain at all but durable earthenware.

Walley's ironstone-type earthenware, with its French nationalist slogans, would have had little attraction for the many Canadians of English descent and sentiments. Maple leaves and beavers, however, were by no means exclusively French-Canadian emblems; they had come to be adopted in the country as a whole. *The Maple Leaf* was the title of one of the earliest of Canada's literary annuals, published in Toronto from 1846. The editor, the Rev. John McCaul, described the publication's name in 1848 as "The chosen emblem of Canada."[8]

The earliest heraldic use of the beaver that can be associated with Canada was not with New France but with New Scotland.[9] Sir William Alexander (Earl of Stirling and Viscount Canada), to whom Nova Scotia was granted by King James I in 1621, made use of the beaver as a crest: "For his crest on a wreath *argent, sable*: a beaver proper." Canada's first postage stamp, designed in 1851 by Sir Sandford Fleming, a Scottish-born Canadian, was the threepenny beaver.

How readily all Canada accepted the twin emblems of the maple leaf and beaver is seen in the annual University Lecture delivered by Principal William Dawson (later Sir William) to the students of McGill University on 27 November 1863. Dawson, one of the most eminent of Canadian educationists and the first president of the Royal Society of Canada, chose as his topic that year "Duties of Educated Young Men in British America." Canada, he told them, "has two emblems ... the *Beaver* and the *Maple*. The beaver in his sagacity, his industry, his ingenuity, and his perseverance, is a most respectable animal; a much better emblem for an infant country than the rapacious eagle or even the lordly lion ..." In the maple, Dawson saw "the vitality and energy of a new country." The maple was "equally at home in the forest" and "in the cultivated field"; in its changing colours it typified the "versatile spirit" needed in an emerging nation.[10]

There was, therefore, a larger patriotic spirit in Canada, symbolized by maple leaves and beavers, on which a potter could capitalize. A firm that did so was Thomas Furnival & Sons of Cobridge. Furnival's pattern, appropriately named "Maple," had a border of the leaves; the beaver formed the central design. Sir William Dawson would have approved of Furnival's beaver. He had deplored the fact that "some of our artists have had the bad taste to represent the beaver as perched on the maple bough; a most unpleasant position for the poor animal."[11] Walley's beaver was so depicted; Furnival's was more realistically on the ground, a spray of maple leaves to one side (Plate 86).

Thomas Furnival & Sons, potting under that business style from 1871 to 1890, was a firm that had strong trade ties with the Canadian market. Canadian importers, never very quick to name the makers of the goods they were selling in the nineteenth century, used, however, to particularize Furnival wares. Edward Hagar's Montreal advertisement of 31 August 1881 not only mentioned Furnival by name but underlined the competition between ironstone-type earthenware and cheap French porcelain:

HANDSOME DINNER SETS,
Of the latest styles, at VERY LOW PRICES.
FURNIVAL WHITE STONE WARE,
Equal in appearance to FRENCH CHINA and more
DURABLE[12]

Furnival's name occurs in surviving business papers of both city merchants and country storekeepers. J.D. Laflamme, for example, owned one of the five general stores in the Ontario village of West Winchester in 1882. On 16 October that year his stock included eight dozen Furnival cups and saucers which he had purchased wholesale in Montreal for ninety cents a dozen.[13]

The Furnival firm also executed special orders for Canada, and one of these was for the legendary North West Mounted Police. For use in the headquarters of the force (transferred from Fort Walsh, in the Cypress Hills of Saskatchewan, to Regina in 1882), Furnival's supplied tough ironstone (or "white stone ware") with the Force's motto, "Maintiens le droit."[14]

It was on the sure foundation of established Canadian demand for their earthenware (both ordinary earthenware and ironstone) that Thomas Furnival & Sons brought out their "Maple" pattern. The shapes of hollow pieces (teapots, jugs, sugar bowls, etc.) indicate an 1880s date for its introduction. This is borne out by the fact that the shape of the vegetable dishes in "Maple" table services was registered at the Patent Office in London on 20 September 1884. The registration number, 13572, appears on a covered vegetable dish in the collections of the National Museum of Man (Plate 87). On these wares, for which a body cream or ivory in tone was most often used (occasionally the

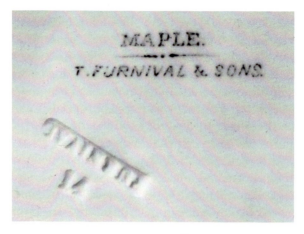

FIGURE 16
"Maple" mark, Furnival & Sons

printing was on a whiter-appearing earthenware) the pattern name was sometimes both printed and impressed on the same piece. The maker's mark (not always present) was T. FURNIVAL & SONS (Figure 16).

An underglaze transfer printed pattern, "Maple" was offered in brown (the colour usually found today), pink, blue (Plate 88), green, or multi-colour (autumn shades). The central beaver was not always present. Small articles, such as ladles (Plate 89), or butter pads, might have only the maple border. "Pad" was the nineteenth-century name for these small items included in many table services sold in Canada from about the mid-1870s.[15] Those in Furnival's "Maple" pattern are usually hexagonal.

The "Maple" pattern was kept in production for a number of years. Copperplates from which it was printed survived at the factory in Staffordshire until the early 1960s, although at the time they were disposed of they had not been in use for at least fifty years. Any wares marked FURNIVALS (instead of T. FURNIVAL & SONS) or with LTD (Limited) in the mark are in date after 1890 and before 1913.[16]

Furnival's "Maple" had none of the limitations of appeal attached to Walley's pattern. Its sale, in what had become the Province of Quebec at the time of Confederation in 1867, would have been to both English and French Canadians. The large amount which has survived in Quebec, as well as in other parts of Canada, is an indication of how astutely Thomas Furnival & Sons judged the market. Theirs was a potters' view of Canada, not in topographical terms, but in terms of patriotic symbolism in the early years of "an infant country."

It was appropriate that one of the original purchasers of the "Maple" pattern should have been a man who had helped to bring Confederation about. The Hon. John

MAPLE LEAVES AND BEAVERS 67

Henry Pope, of Cookshire in the Eastern Townships of Quebec, had a brown-printed table service of Furnival's "Maple." Not only was Pope a cabinet minister under Sir John A. Macdonald, he had played an important role in the negotiations that brought Macdonald and his bitter political opponent, George Brown, together to launch the movement for the Confederation of British North America. Since John Henry Pope died in 1889, only a few years after the Furnival firm introduced its earthenware decorated with Canada's twin emblems, he must have been among the early purchasers of the pattern.[17]

CHAPTER TEN

Canadian Sports

"To any healthy man, woman or child, a Canadian Winter
... is an exhilirating tonic."
W. George Beers, 1883

The zest and excitement of Canadian sports, particularly winter sports, inspired a multi-scene pattern on Scottish earthenware of the 1880s. The maker was John Marshall & Co. of Bo'ness.

In Great Britain winter was often depicted by artists as a bitter experience. Sheep huddled together in driving snow conjured up thoughts of nature's cruelty; waifs too thinly clad for freezing temperatures or old men forlornly driving cattle along snow-rutted lanes were familiar subjects. Canadians, whose winters were cold beyond the wildest imagining of many in the old land, experienced, none the less, an exhilaration in that season. As one Canadian declared, "To any healthy man, woman or child, a Canadian Winter ... is an exhilirating [sic] tonic."[1] It was the winter sports that enhanced the sense of exhilaration. In the 1880s the most popular were skating, snowshoeing, and tobogganing. Anyone was free to take part. Governors-general, garrison officers, newly arrived immigrants, all looked on in wonder at first and then quickly joined in the fun.

Sir William Howard Russell, the celebrated correspondent of the London *Times*, recorded an amusing instance of the newcomer's reaction when he paid a winter visit to Montreal in the 1860s. He spent an afternoon at the Victoria Skating Rink watching good-looking girls "gliding, swooping, revolving" on the ice. On the sidelines, their eyes glued to the "mighty pretty sight," was a cluster of "newly arrived officers" enviously "sucking their canes" and resolving to begin skating lessons the next day.[2]

The newest immigrants, even those with little money in their pockets, were able to enjoy winter amusements. Sarah Thompson, who came to Canada from England in 1857, with her husband and two young sons, wrote home to her sisters that the boys had made "handsleighs" for themselves at the first snowfall and had taken her for a moonlight run through the snow. She felt a sense of almost breathless elation as she was dragged along "at an amazing rate."[3] George Beers, the noted Montreal snowshoer and the writer who described the Canadian winter as a "tonic," advised all "grumblers" to stop cooping themselves up around a stove in the winter months and get out in Canada's brilliant sunshine, where the snow "sparkles ... like a forest of diamonds" and tobogganers go "tearing ... along like highway comets."[4]

It was this lively, healthy aspect of Canadian life that many an immigrant, settling in well, wanted to convey to friends and family across the ocean. In the last quarter of the century, when the fashion for exchanging Christmas and New Year's cards gathered momentum, prompting Canadian publishers to produce cards of their own, winter sports were prominently featured. "Just the Cards to send to your friends in Britain," and "Don't forget to send home a set" were typical advertisements for cards depicting Canadian winter activities.[5] Unexpectedly, there is a direct link between these Victorian greeting cards and the Scottish potter's views of Canada, for the views that appeared on John Marshall & Co.'s earthenware were views published by William Bennet & Co. of Montreal as Christmas and New Year's cards. Because they were adapted for pottery decoration, the date when the cards were introduced becomes important to the historian and china collector.

Several factors determine the date. Montreal city directories indicate that Bennet & Co., whose name appears in that form on the front of the cards, were active from 1877 to 1887. The firm was variously listed as printers, stationers, and representatives of Quebec paper mills. It may have been the same firm that was listed briefly and appeared occasionally in advertisements in the 1860s (a *Daily Witness* advertisement of 19 December 1867 mentions "Bennett's [sic] News Rooms"), but in the 1860s the Christmas card industry was not yet sufficiently developed for Canadians to venture on cards of their own. There were very few advertisements for Christmas cards of any kind in Canada in the 1860s. Not until about the mid-1870s did advertisements begin to proliferate and Canadian subjects begin to come to the fore. Cards published by "Bennet & Co. Montreal" were, therefore, from the firm active under that business style for approximately ten years, beginning towards the end of the 1870s. Within that decade the date can be narrowed further. Some of the costumes suggest a date in the 1880s, rather than the 1870s. The skating girl on one of the cards, for example, wears a costume very similar to a costume illustrated as the newest fashion for skaters in *Cassell's Family Magazine* for January 1880. The most conclusive evidence, however, for an 1880s date of publication for the Montreal cards comes from those who originally received and preserved them. In three known instances cards in Bennet & Co.'s Canadian sports series are dated 1882, either written in ink on the back of the card or beside it in an old scrapbook. Their theme appealing in Canada as well as abroad, these three cards were originally received by persons living in the Province of Quebec. Grace Collard of Montreal was one of the recipients. Her card depicted the skating girl and on the back she noted: "From Nelly ... Xmas 1882" (Plate 90). She similarly annotated other cards received that year, tied them all up with a ribbon, and placed them in the bottom compartment of an old rosewood writing box. They remained undisturbed for close to a century. In 1968 the cards annotated by Grace Collard almost ninety years earlier were found when the box was inherited by a descendant. Her skating girl was the first clue to the source of John Marshall & Co.'s "Canadian Sports" pattern.[6]

In dating the introduction of Bennet & Co.'s sports cards it is, perhaps, not without significance that 1882 was a year in which the firm's business was booming, with orders coming in "not only from all parts of the Dominion" but even from the United States.[7] It is also relevant that in the 1880s both retailers and publishers constantly stressed new designs in cards each season. "I never offer my customers old cards ... nothing but the newest of the new" was a typical advertisement by a Montreal publisher.[8]

Bennet & Co.'s cards were "published" in Montreal. Who designed them and where they were lithographed in colour is not known. Not all the cards put out by Canadian publishers were produced in Canada. Many were printed in England or Germany. The backgrounds in the Bennet series are more European than Canadian. Also unknown is how many cards made up the complete set of Canadian sports. To date seven, each with a subject also found on earthenware, have come to light.

John Marshall, the Scottish potter who made use of these Canadian scenes, acquired the pottery at Borrowstounness (Bo'ness) in Lowland Scotland in the 1850s. According to Llewellynn Jewitt, he took William McNay as a partner in 1867 and the firm then became J. Marshall & Co.[9] Marshall died within a few years, but the pottery was continued under the old name until the end of the century.[10]

The "Canadian Sports" pattern was brought out in the 1880s. The date for its introduction is set not only by the Bennet & Co. cards, but also by the shapes of hollow pieces in the pattern. Teapots, for instance, are identical in shape to other Marshall & Co. teapots that can be firmly placed in the 1880s. The collections of the National Museum of Man include a Marshall & Co. teapot in a printed floral pattern that carries a registration mark for the beginning of the 1880s. It is identical in size and shape to teapots in "Canadian Sports." Large jugs, which come in several sizes and shapes in "Canadian Sports," are sometimes in forms more usually associated with the later 1880s. The pattern was probably in production for some years, beginning shortly before or just about the middle of the decade.

The earthenware body used by J. Marshall & Co. for "Canadian Sports" was most often of the cream or ivory tone popular in the mid-1880s, but like the "Maple" pattern of Thomas Furnival & Sons, also introduced at this period, "Canadian Sports" was occasionally printed on a body distinctly white. The underglaze transfer printing was generally in black, sometimes in brown, or (rarest of all) in blue. The pattern, with floral border, was also offered with added colour (pink, blue, green, yellow) over black printing. Gilding was occasionally used on rims and handles.

For some Canadian collectors the identification of the maker of this pattern seems in the past to have presented curious and needless difficulties. There should never have been any real mystery about it. A proportion of what was sold in Canada was marked with the pattern name ("Canadian Sports"), the maker's initials or name (J. M. & CO., or J. MARSHALL & CO. in full), and sometimes also with the key word BO'NESS or BO'NESS POTTERY (impressed within a device). The pattern name was usually printed, the

FIGURE 17
J.M. & Co. printed mark

maker's initials or name printed or impressed (Figure 17). It is true that much of this ware was unmarked, but it would be difficult to make any representative collection of "Canadian Sports" over any reasonable length of time without coming upon at least one marked specimen. The products of John Marshall & Co. were described in obvious reference books published as long ago as Llewellynn Jewitt's indispensable *The Ceramic Art of Great Britain* (1878) and Arnold Fleming's *Scottish Pottery* (1923). The connection between "Canadian Sports" and J. Marshall & Co. was clearly established in *Nineteenth-Century Pottery and Porcelain in Canada* in 1967.[11]

Dinner, tea, and toilet sets were made in "Canadian Sports" (Plate 91). As in all multi-scene patterns, different views appeared on different articles, but the same view did not always appear on the same article. Teapots usually had a tobogganer on one side (skaters on the other), but the tobogganer was sometimes a boy lying full length on his toboggan (Plate 92), sometimes a daring young woman recklessly standing as she rushes down a hill. Cups in a tea set displayed various views. On large articles, such as ewers and basins or meat dishes, as many as five or six views (reduced in size) might appear.

The seven views on earthenware that correspond to the seven known Bennet & Co. Christmas and New Year's cards are: the skating girl; a scene in which a young man kneels to adjust his female companion's snowshoes (Plate 93); a male snowshoer striding along (Plates 94, 96); a child with a snow shovel (Plates 95, 97); a scene with two children on a sled (Plates 98, 99); another skating scene, with male skaters (Plates 100, 101); and, finally, the fearless woman tobogganer (Plates 102, 103). It seems likely that all the views making up "Canadian Sports" on earthenware had their counterparts in the Bennet & Co. cards, and that in time more of these cards will come to light.

In addition to the views now listed as appearing also on the Montreal-published cards, those on Scottish earthenware include still another snowshoeing scene (Plate 104). In this one, male snowshoers attempt to negotiate a rail fence with what appears to be barbed wire off to one side. Barbed wire was patented in 1873, but was not a common sight in Canada until a few years later.[12] By 1883, however (the approximate date of the Marshall & Co. scene), barbed wire had become common enough to be regarded as a hazard by sports enthusiasts.[13]

Although the majority of the scenes in the "Canadian Sports" pattern are of winter amusements, there are at least two of lacrosse players (Plates 105, 106). Lacrosse could be, and sometimes was played on the ice, but it was normally considered a summer sport. On earthenware it is depicted in a summer setting. In the 1870s and 1880s lacrosse was extremely popular and when, in 1876, two Canadian teams (one of Indians from Caughnawaga) toured Great Britain, something of the spell of what was then Canada's national game swept the British Isles. English crowds watched breathlessly as Indians, swift as the wind, demonstrated their skill in the game they had originated, and marvelled that goalkeepers seemed willing to be smashed and maimed rather than permit an opponent to score. Even Queen Victoria was caught up in the excitement. She commanded the Canadians to play before her and afterwards presented them with her photograph.

One of the scenes in "Canadian Sports" was entirely incongruous, having nothing to do with sports at all. A little girl feeding a goose made a surprising appearance on plates and jugs (Plate 107). Her activity could scarcely be called a Canadian sport, but interpolations of this kind were accepted without question. Marshall & Co.'s little girl and her goose were no more out of keeping than the fanciful European lake scene that Francis Morley injected into his Canadian views adapted from Bartlett.

One small plate in the collections of the National Musuem of Man differs from other examples of the "Canadian Sports" pattern in that its border is not the usual printed border but a moulded one, divided into compartments and featuring sprays of shamrocks (Plate 104). The scene in the centre, printed in brown, is the amusing one in which a male snowshoer meets his Waterloo at a fence. It is tempting to speculate that this small plate may have had some connection with the Emerald Snowshoe Club (one of Montreal's major clubs, flourishing in the 1880s and with a membership composed mainly of Irishmen). It may, however, have been intended as nothing more than a small plate to amuse a child.

Marshall & Co.'s "Canadian Sports," unlike some of the potters' views of Canada, was brought out with the Canadian market in mind. It used to be found not infrequently in the Eastern Townships of Quebec and in eastern Ontario. In bringing out a Canadian pattern, the Scottish firm was in the same position as the Staffordshire potters, Podmore, Walker & Co. and Francis Morley & Co. A trade with Canada had already been well established before Canadian views were attempted. One of Marshall & Co.'s patterns that undoubtedly helped pave the way for "Canadian Sports" was an idealized scene to which the name "Bosphorus" was given.[14] Most of what the Bo'ness Pottery sent to Canada was for the country trade. The "Bosphorus" pattern is one of those mentioned in the business papers of J.D. Laflamme, a country storekeeper in

Ontario.[15] That "Canadian Sports" also belonged, at least in part, to the same country or lower-priced market is shown by the existence of "seconds" (articles that left the pottery in imperfect condition and were retailed at less than "firsts": "SECONDS means CULLS," said a Canadian advertisement of Victorian times).[16] "Seconds" might be sold in urban areas to those who wanted cheap goods, but it was the country stores that absorbed much of this class of crockery and it was at city trade sales of "Crockery suitable for Country Stores" (as a Montreal advertisement of 1867 put it) that these "culls" were largely offered.[17] It is possible to find plates in "Canadian Sports" so badly potted that they may be spun like tops.

Although "Canadian Sports" was introduced with the Canadian market primarily in mind, it should be noted that a certain amount of the pattern was also sold in the British Isles. It is found from time to time in Scotland itself and also in Ireland. Both the greeting cards from Canada and these potter's views would have appealed to "friends in Britain." Anyone who had watched, fascinated, the visiting Canadians furiously playing lacrosse, or who had joined one of the British teams that sprang up in the wake of the Canadians' tour, would have been a potential customer for jugs and plates and cups printed with scenes of this Canadian sport.

When compared with such potters' views of Canada as Enoch Wood & Sons' Table Rock, Montmorency, or Quebec, or Davenport's picture of the *British America* and Montreal, John Marshall & Co.'s Canadian sports scenes have a rough and primitive appearance; they are less sophisticated in execution. Yet there is about them a naïve attraction. They bring back days when Canadian girls in velvet toques and sweeping skirts darted over the ice with an ease that amazed envious visitors; when snowshoers strode swiftly forward with "tassels flying picturesquely in the wind"; when tobogganers hurtled down hills as if "thrown from a catapult."[18] What George Beers called the bone-bred love of open air sports was responsible not only for a set of Victorian greeting cards but for a Scottish potter's views of Canada.

CHAPTER ELEVEN

Photographs and the Potter

"... places of interest in and about old Quebec ..."
C.E. Holiwell, 1889

Mary FitzGibbon, writing at the end of the 1870s and describing "the 'best room' of most Canadian farmhouses," noted that the few books almost always included "a Bible, almanac, and photograph album."[1] The photograph album was already well on its way to becoming a familiar object in Canadian city houses as early as the 1860s, sharing the drawing room table with books of engravings such as Bartlett's *Canadian Scenery*.[2] By 1880, the year Mary FitzGibbon's Canadian travel book was published, the engravings had been all but displaced, in town and country, by the photograph album. It was the photograph album that characters in fiction now toyed with. The "handsome young fellow" in chapter 1 of a serial, beginning in the *Canadian Monthly* in July 1879, was idly "turning over the pages of a large album of photographs" as he listened to piano music in "the Doctor's little drawing-room."[3] An album of photographs, said a writer in a popular magazine of 1880, had become "one of the common objects" in every house.[4] It was, therefore, to be expected that the potters' views of Canada in the later years of the century would include topographical views based on photographs.

Not long after Mary FitzGibbon commented on the ubiquitousness of the photograph album in Canadian homes, a Scottish pottery brought out a multi-scene pattern on earthenware, using as the source of the printed decoration photographs of Quebec City and its environs. The pottery was Robert Cochran's Britannia Pottery in the St Rollox district of Glasgow. The Quebec views, however, were only occasionally marked with the maker's name. They had been ordered by a Quebec City china merchant, Francis T. Thomas, and the mark that normally appeared on them was F.T. THOMAS / QUEBEC (printed underglaze on the back).

Thomas was one of the most enterprising Canadian china merchants of the last quarter of the nineteenth century. He had been an employee of a Quebec importing firm (McCaghey, Dolbec & Co.). In 1874, when his employers ran into financial difficulties, he took over their premises in Quebec's Lower Town and went into business for himself. He prospered quickly. In January 1881 the *Mercantile Agency Reference Book* gave him a credit rating of "Good"; by September 1887, it had climbed to "High." Though Thomas died in 1897, his business continued, becoming the Thomas Company Limited in the twentieth century.[5]

Of all the china merchants in Canada in the nineteenth century, Thomas was the only one to commission table services and toilet sets with Canadian topographical views. Unfortunately, the fact that his name appeared on them was later to cause confusion. When collectors first became interested in potters' views of Canada, enthusiasts jumped to the conclusion that Thomas was the potter and the wares had been made in Quebec. The myth persisted for a surprising number of years – among some collectors, at least. Yet no one with any knowledge of the state of Canadian potting in the 1880s, when the Quebec views were introduced, could have supposed a Canadian potter responsible for them. It is true that Thomas was concerned with a local pottery, but it was not a pottery capable of making white-bodied earthenware decorated with accomplished underglaze transfer printing. No pottery in Canada, not even the well-known St Johns Stone Chinaware Co., was attempting such wares as these Quebec views in the 1880s.

The Quebec views were made in Scotland. The factory that received the order for them had a long connection with the Canadian market. The Britannia Pottery was one of two operated by Robert Cochran, a one-time Glasgow china merchant of boundless energy and sound business judgment. In the 1840s he had acquired the Verreville Pottery in Finnieston (then outside Glasgow); in the 1850s he planned a new pottery, the Britannia, in St Rollox (the north-east district of Glasgow). When finally completed – it took some years – the Britannia was one of the largest in Scotland, with the most modern equipment (the noise of its thundering machinery was said to be absolutely deafening). Even in an age of rapid industrial progress, the Britannia Pottery's capacity was staggering: "One thousand dozens of plates, and as many cups and saucers were turned out daily, besides other articles."[6]

To promote sales in Canada, Cochran sent out agents. Long before Francis Thomas entered the china, glass, and earthenware business in Quebec, printed wares from the Britannia Pottery had been distributed far and wide in British North America. Idealized scenes with such pattern names as "Syria" and "Damascus" had prepared the way for Canadian scenes.

When Cochran died in 1869 the Britannia Pottery passed into the hands of his younger son, Alexander. This only strengthened the tie with Canada; for Alexander had as his managing partner James (later Sir James) Fleming who, as a young man, had crossed to Canada on a sailing ship to drum up business for Robert Cochran.[7] The link with Canada had been firmly forged. Francis Thomas would have been handling the Britannia's products before he gave the order for the printed pattern of Quebec views that was to carry his own name.

The date when this order was given could not have been earlier than 1879, since one of the views was of the Dufferin Terrace, completed only that year (Plate 108). It was opened on 9 June by the Marquis of Lorne, Governor-General of Canada. Lord Lorne's wife Princess Louise, a daughter of Queen Victoria, accompanied her husband to Quebec and together they headed a procession which "promenaded the new terrace." Lord Lorne then formally declared it open and named for his predecessor in office, Lord Dufferin.[8] The terrace, more than a quarter of a mile in length and 182 feet above the St Lawrence, became one of the great scenic boardwalks of the world. The photograph which was the basis for the pottery view could not have been taken before the late spring of 1879 (there is no ice or snow in evidence). It was very likely taken about the time the terrace was opened (Plate 109). The earthenware would not have been on sale in Canada before 1880 at the earliest. That it was on sale in 1881 has been stated by Marius Barbeau: "A full set in dull rose ... was purchased of Francis Thomas in 1881."[9] This "full set" would seem to have been the one Barbeau referred to elsewhere as having been given to his parents as a wedding present.[10]

There are numerous records of the popularity of this tableware for wedding presents in the Quebec area. Early in the 1890s another set in the same "dull rose" was presented to Désiré Octeau by his bachelor friends on the eve of his marriage. It was inherited by his granddaughter, and today part of this table service is in the collections of the National Museum of Man. Francis Thomas had judged well when he ordered views of Quebec printed on ivory-toned earthenware from Scotland. For these potters' views of Canada there was such a constant demand that the pattern remained in production well into the present century. It was still being made as late as the 1920s.

The twentieth-century wares were usually more thinly potted than those of the 1880s and the body somewhat whiter. The maker's mark, when present, is a guide to date. Prior to 1896 the name COCHRAN might appear on the wares (Figure 18). In the McCord Museum of McGill University is one of the "pulls," or proofs, from the copperplates for these views. It is from a set sent out to Thomas in Quebec from the pottery in Scotland, and it shows both Thomas' own mark (as the importer) and the marker's name: COCHRAN ST ROLLOX. In 1896 the business style of the firm changed. According to Arnold Fleming, son of James Fleming, it then became COCHRAN & FLEMING. A few years later Alexander Cochran died. The Flemings, father and son, then ran the business. From 1911 to 1920 Arnold Fleming was in charge, his father having retired. The mark COCHRAN & FLEMING dates from 1896 into the early twentieth century; the mark FLEMING alone is probably after the turn of the century. In 1920 the pottery was sold to the Britannia Pottery Co. Ltd., and the change was reflected in the marks (Figure 19).[11] The collections of the National Museum of Man include a plate in this series of views with the mark: B.P. CO. LTD. MADE IN SCOTLAND (surrounding a figure of Britannia).

The printing of the Quebec views was most often in brown (sometimes a slightly darker brown on the later products). The pattern was also offered in pink (what Barbeau called "a dull rose"). On some of the twentieth-century examples the "dull rose" became a very pale pink. The views have also been reported in pale blue.

The border was composed of patriotic symbols: beavers and maple leaves en-

FIGURE 18
Cochran's "Quebec" mark

twined with roses, shamrocks, and thistles. Dinner, tea, and toilet wares were all offered – everything from egg cups to tooth-brush holders. Teapots, cream jugs, and covered sugar bowls were in what was frequently advertised in the closing years of the century as the "New Square Shape."[12] In this, the Britannia teaware was akin to the same articles in Thomas Furnival & Sons' "Maple" pattern.

The Quebec views differed from the earlier topographical views of Canada not only in being derived from photographs but in the way in which the scenes were identified: on the front of each piece and not on the back, as were Enoch Wood's view of Quebec and Podmore, Walker & Co.'s views after Bartlett. Moreover, with one or two exceptions, the identification was in both English and French.

In all, almost twenty different views were used by the Britannia Pottery for their "Quebec" pattern. They included:

Dufferin Terrace & Citadel. Place Dufferin & Citadelle (Plates 108, 109)
St Louis Gate. Porte St. Louis (Plates 110, 111)
St John's Gate. Porte St. Jean (Plates 112, 113)
Quebec Harbor & Levis. Hâvre de Québec & Levis (Plates 114, 115)
Quebec from Point Levis. Québec, vue de Point Levis (Plate 116)
View Looking North from the Citadel. Vue prise de la Citadelle (Plate 117)
Wolfe's Monument. Monument de Wolfe (Plate 118)
Wolfe & Montcalm Monument. Monument de Wolfe & Montcalm (Plate 119)
Basilica & Seminary. Basilique & Séminaire (Plate 120)
Chaudière Falls. Chûtes de la Chaudière (Plate 121)

FIGURE 19
Mark on later "Quebec" wares

Natural Steps, Montmorency River. Marches Naturelles, Rivière Montmorency
  (Plates 122, 123)
Cape Diamond. Cap Diamant (Plates 124, 125)
Lorette Falls. Chûtes de Lorette (Plate 126)
Montmorency Fall. Chûte de Montmorency (Plates 127, 128)
Montmorency Fall. Winter View. (No French title) (Plate 129)
Abraham Hill. (No French title) (Plates 130, 131)
Breakneck Steps. Escalier Champlain (Plate 132)
An untitled picture featuring an Indian squaw (Plates 133, 134)
An untitled picture featuring an Indian chief (Plates 135, 136)

All these scenes are represented in the collections of the National Museum of
Man. The source of the scenes was obviously photographs, a fact borne out by the
discovery of a small booklet entitled *Quebec* and composed of views of Quebec and its
environs derived from photographs.[13] The thirty views in the booklet included all but
one of the views known on earthenware. As usual, the pottery engraver had made some
changes, but the views in the booklet and the views on the earthenware corresponded in
such remarkable detail that the link between them was indisputable. The changes
involved mainly thinning out figures in a crowded scene or dropping a sailing ship or
two from a harbour view. A pottery engraver would be conscious of the fact that too
many small figures or ships might, after the earthenware was glazed and fired, result in
mere blobs or dots. To fill up white space the pottery engraver – again as was usual in
such cases – added cloud effects. But not only did the views themselves correspond in

extraordinary detail, the bilingual captions under the pictures in the booklet were the same captions that appeared under the views on the earthenware. Here, in this booklet, was evidence of the source of the earthenware views.

The discovery of the booklet, published and copyrighted by Charles E. Holiwell, a Quebec City engraver, printer, and stationer who had been in business since the 1860s, did not, however, answer all questions about the source of the pottery views. In the first place, the booklet had been copyrighted in 1888.[14] The earthenware was on the market a little earlier. In the second place, Holiwell was not himself a photographer. He advertised as a dealer in: "PHOTOGRAPHS OF ALL SIZES of the different places of interest in and about old Quebec ..."[15] It seemed clear, therefore, that Holiwell had gathered together a collection of photographs which he had probably been selling as individual items for some time before he decided to publish them. There was no clue in the booklet as to whose work he had published, but Ralph Greenhill, an authority on early Canadian photography, has identified the photographer of most, if not indeed all of the views, as Louis Prudent Vallée.[16] Vallée had studied photography in New York, then returned to work in Quebec in the 1860s (the same time Holiwell was setting up in business). He was active for the rest of the century, his working years more or less paralleling Holiwell's.

The two pictures that appear on earthenware without identification (Plates 133, 135), the Indian woman and the Indian man, both of which were used on cups, are in Holiwell's *Quebec*. The captions there are:

Lorette Squaw. "Sauvagesse" de Lorette

Indian Chief. Chef Sauvage

The one view on earthenware not in the Holiwell album of 1888 is "Abraham Hill," which occurs on jugs (Plate 130). The border on these jugs differs from the regular "Quebec" border. It is a narrow band (around the rim of the jugs) of roses, shamrocks, and thistles only. That the jugs belong with the "Quebec" pattern, in spite of the oddity of the border, is evident from the fact they are regularly found with teaware in this pattern. This jug, for example, went with the tea and table service given to Désiré Octeau at the dinner held in his honour the night before his wedding. No other jug accompanied the various articles of teaware in that presentation service for twelve. Although "Abraham Hill" was not included in Holiwell's 1888 publication, the view on the jug was taken almost unchanged from a Vallée photograph (Plate 131). Vallée specialized in stereographs and "Abraham Hill" was no. 70 in a series he called "Canadian Scenery." ("ALWAYS ON HAND, VIEWS OF QUEBEC" was printed on the back of the stereograph, together with Vallée's name, address on St John Street, and the title of the series.)

Holiwell published more than one "Album" (as he described them).[17] There is another copyrighted in 1892. This later one dropped the pictures of the Indian woman and Indian chief and added others. It is possible that Holiwell published more than these two albums.

That Vallée and Holiwell had some business arrangement is plain. Vallée himself issued a catalogue of his photographs that included, with English titles, views used on earthenware. This catalogue may have preceded anything published by Holiwell.[18] Both Vallée and Holiwell, it is worth noting, sought the tourist trade. Vallée described his photographs as "respectfully presented to the tourist visiting Quebec." Holiwell's albums were in handy small size and included useful maps for the tourist. His little albums were, in fact, tourists' souvenirs in themselves. When the views on earthenware are examined, it becomes clear that they are a tourist itinerary of the "places of interest in and about old Quebec." The photographs and stereographs by Vallée, the albums by Holiwell, and the earthenware views were all on sale in Quebec in the 1880s and 1890s. Each would have promoted the others, not only in the tourist trade but in the local trade. The photographs and albums could adorn the Quebec drawing room or parlour table at the same time as the earthenware was set out in the dining room.

Whether Francis Thomas went to Vallée for the photographs he sent to Glasgow to be worked up for printing on earthenware, or whether he purchased them as individual items from Holiwell, is impossible to say. What is important to the china collector is the fact these views of Quebec and its environs were the basis for the transfer-printed pattern made at the Britannia Pottery in Scotland and sold by Francis Thomas in Quebec.

In the 1860s a Quebec newspaper advertisement spoke of "the truthfulness of Photography."[19] The nineteenth-century potters who had used the artist's emotional interpretations of Canadian views turned, in the closing years of the century, to the literal. The scenes might be the same, but they looked at them in a new way. For many Victorians, for whom progress was change, and who welcomed every new invention with excited awe, photography was but another step in what they regarded as the improvement of the quality and variety of human achievement. The days of the search for sublimity and for the romantic had faded. The day of the "truthful" photograph had arrived, even in the potters' views of Canada.

QUEBEC

CHAPTER TWELVE

Miscellaneous Canadian Views

"CROCKERY ... a ... varied assortment."
Montreal *Argus*, 12 May 1857

The earliest of the potters' views of Canada that comes under the classification of miscellaneous is one of Quebec taken from the opposite shore (Plate 137). In date it belongs to the early 1830s and is, therefore, of about the same period as Enoch Wood & Sons' view of the same scene approached from the same angle, but interpreted differently. Both were printed in the same dark blue. This second view, however, has no maker's mark.

Those resident in British America in the 1830s considered the old walled city of Quebec one of "the most romantic" sights "in the Canadas." Quebec, said the writer of a Canadian guidebook published in 1831, offered "a rich treat ... a *coup d'œil* hardly surpassed on earth."[1] Alfred Hawkins, the shipping master of the port, declared in 1834 that Quebec's position was "unique ... in natural sublimity it stands, as to the cities of the continent, unrivalled and alone." The "majestic" appearance of Cape Diamond, the "purest silver" of the St Lawrence, the blaze and sparkle of the whole scene made the city a never-to-be-forgotten sight, and among the most impressive the world could offer.[2]

In spite of the appreciation of Quebec's picturesque beauties expressed by those living there in the 1830s, and who might have been expected to become eager buyers of a Quebec view on tableware, the Staffordshire potter responsible for this view unquestionably intended it for sale not in Canada but in the United States. Printed in a colour that sold well in the American market, the Quebec scene was part of a series depicting towns and cities. Nearly all were in the United States, the principal exceptions being Quebec and Buenos Aires. Quebec's companions in the series included Albany, Baltimore, Cincinnati, Detroit, Washington, and such American sights as a ferry on the

Susquehanna and William Penn's treaty tree (under which the founder of Pennsylvania made a treaty with the Indians). If further proof were needed that this potter's view of Quebec was intended primarily for sale in the United States it is found in the names of American importers recorded on a number of the views. A Cincinnati dealer's name has been recorded on the Quebec view, and the names of dealers in New Orleans, Louisville, and Wheeling on others.[3]

Each view was identified on the back of the earthenware. No maker's mark was added, but the series is now attributed by collectors in the United States to the Staffordshire firm of James and Ralph Clews. The attribution has been made on the strength of a bowl with the Quebec view which has both the floral border regularly used in this series and an added border corresponding to one used by the Clews brothers on a series of views illustrating ceramically the story of Don Quixote.[4] Contrary to what is sometimes stated, Staffordshire potters did borrow borders. It would set all hesitations at rest to find a fully marked specimen of the city series, but in further support of the Clews attribution there is the fact that one of the views (taken near Fishkill on the Hudson River) was used by the Clews firm in another, and marked, series which had the general pattern name of "Picturesque Views."[5]

If James and Ralph Clews were the makers of the Quebec view, then it would have to date no later than the mid-1830s. The brothers, who had been potting together since, or just shortly before, 1818, were bankrupt by 1835.[6] One of the views in the series (Albany) was based on an engraving published in 1831.[7] The American importers whose names have been found on the wares were all dealers active in the early 1830s. A number of factors, therefore, in addition to the appearance of the wares, point to a date in the first half of the 1830s for earthenware with this view of Quebec.

But although the tea, coffee, and dinner wares printed with the Quebec scene were made in the 1830s, the source of the view was not necessarily of that date. The Clews brothers may have drawn, either directly or indirectly, on "A General View of Quebec from Point Levy," published in London in 1761 (Plate 138). A British naval officer, Richard Short, was the artist. He had been present at the capture of Quebec by General Wolfe in 1759, and this particular view was one of a series of drawings he made "on the spot." Short's view and the view on earthenware have features in common, notably the stone house and the great tree at the left of the scene, but if the left half of Short's view was, in fact, the source from which the pottery artist worked, then he exerted to the full his right to make changes. He omitted, for example, the two British Grenadiers and other soldiers in Short's foreground (the two figures he put in may or may not have been intended as sailors). He also omitted all the soldiers at the water line, and altered the shipping on the river.

Whatever the source, the scene entitled "Quebec," in a device on the back (Figure 20), was of an actual place. Very different, and at least a decade later, is the idealized view named (on the back) "Ontario Lake Scenery" (Plate 139). It earns its place among the potters' views of Canada by virtue of its name, not its reality.

The maker of "Ontario Lake Scenery" was the Staffordshire potter, Joseph Heath, in business from the mid-1840s to the early 1850s. Tea (Plate 140), dinner, and

FIGURE 20
"Quebec" (city series) mark

toilet wares were made in this pattern and printed underglaze in light blue, brown, pink, mauve, or (occasionally) in green. Heath's mark occurs in two forms, printed and impressed, the two often on the same piece. The printed mark accompanies an ornamental device enclosing the pattern name (Figure 21). On some wares (for example, on a pink-printed plate in the collections of the National Museum of Man) the ornamental device and pattern name are accompanied not by Heath's name but by the initials B & D (Figure 22). What the initials stand for is not clear. Used together in this way, they do not seem to fit any recorded potter of the period.

A possible, but entirely speculative explanation of the initials B & D might be that they are an exporter's or importer's mark. If so, an analogy could be drawn with another obscure mark, MT & CO., which is found on a printed pattern named "Delhi" (in date c. 1850). "Delhi" was sold in impressive quantities in Canada, particularly in the Eastern Townships of Quebec, where at one time it used to turn up regularly at house auctions. Jacob Niles Galer, a nineteenth-century businessman in the village of Dunham, was one who had a table service in this pattern.[8] As with the B & D mark, the initials MT & CO. fitted no recorded maker. The puzzle was partially solved in 1979 when a saucer was found in Ottawa bearing the impressed mark of the Staffordshire potter, Joseph Clementson, as well as the printed MT & CO. mark, and the pattern name. MT & CO., by this token, appear to have been the sellers of "Delhi" tableware made by Clementson, a potter who strenuously cultivated the Canadian trade.[9]

In naming his pattern "Ontario Lake Scenery," Heath must have had the lake and not the province in mind. When the pattern was introduced, what is now the Province of Ontario was officially Canada West. Older people probably still called it Upper Canada.

FIGURE 21
"Ontario Lake Scenery" mark

Victorian potters frequently gave names of actual places to idealized scenes, even to patterns that could not be called "views" of any kind. Edward Walley, the Staffordshire potter who made wares printed with maple leaves, beavers, and French-Canadian nationalist slogans, also sent out to Canada a pattern printed in blue or pink called "Ontario." The scene had nothing to do with Ontario, lake or province, it was another fanciful view.[10] Samuel Alcock, potting in Burslem from the 1830s to the end of the 1850s, gave the name "Toronto" to blue, green, or brown-printed earthenware with a geometrical design as the central decoration.[11] J. Dimmock & Co. of Hanley supplied a printed floral pattern (again, in blue, green, or brown) to Boxer Brothers & Co., Montreal importers in the 1880s, and called it "Montreal."

In this same decade (the 1880s), the Staffordshire firm of Wallis Gimson & Co. of Fenton brought out a multi-scene pattern entitled "The World." Registered at the Patent Office in London on 27 May 1884 (design no. 7624), it reflected the prevailing influence of Japanese design, in that the general composition was asymmetrical and included what one writer termed the inevitable "little ... views ... at the side."[12] These "little views," set within frames (square, circular, diamond-shaped) and placed off-centre, provided glimpses of notable buildings and scenery around the world. Among the Canadian scenes were: the Grand Battery at Quebec (Plate 141); Wolfe's Monument, Quebec; the Band Stand, Quebec; Notre Dame Church, Montreal (Plate 142); the Lieutenant-Governor's Residence, Toronto; the Normal School, Toronto (Plate 143); the University of Toronto; Niagara Falls, winter and summer views (Plate 144); the Governor-General's Residence (Rideau Hall), Ottawa; and the federal Parliament Buildings, Ottawa (Plate 142). Each scene was identified on the face of the piece.

FIGURE 22
Unidentified B & D mark

Flowers arranged in what the British potters conceived to be the Japanese style completed the design. The British potters' aim, during the years of the "Japanese mania," which swept over the western world in the later nineteenth century, was not "servile imitations" but, as Llewellynn Jewitt explained it at the time, to produce "original designs imbued with the quaint ideas of the Japanese ... rendered more ... acceptable by the refinement of feeling of the English mind."[13]

The border used with this pattern was composed of demi-florettes above a narrow chain effect. The underglaze printing on the earthenware was most often in brown, occasionally in a bluish-green, sometimes in a two-colour printing of brown and green. On the most expensive of the wares the flowers were given natural colours (including yellow, pink, and blue) and gilding was added to rims and handles. The shapes of hollow pieces were very like the "New Square Shape" used for the Britannia Pottery's "Quebec" or Thomas Furnival & Sons' "Maple" pattern, and as with these wares of the same period, the earthenware was generally of an ivory tone.

The maker's name, the firm's trade mark (a beehive), the registration number, and the pattern name were all printed on the back of many pieces. On some, the name or initials of a seller, not the maker's name, appeared. An example is the mark on a large brown-printed meat dish in the collections of the National Museum of Man: in place of Wallis Gimson & Co.'s name are the words, "MANUFACTURED FOR PRIMAVESI & SONS SWANSEA." Gimson & Co. were in business from 1883 to 1890 (not from 1884, as is usually stated).[14] The pattern may have been in production during the entire life of the firm.

One of the views in "The World" pattern, the "University of Toronto" (as it was titled), is found on octagonal plates on which the second "framed" picture is a portrait of the Prince of Wales (later King Edward VII). On the back of these plates is printed the information that they were issued on the occasion of "the Prince of Wales' visit." Whatever these plates commemorated, it was not, as has been sometimes said, a visit of the prince to Canada in the 1880s. The Prince of Wales was in Canada only once, in 1860, when the primary object of his visit was to open the Victoria Bridge over the St Lawrence at Montreal. There was a suggestion that the prince come to Canada in 1883, but although the rumour of such a visit was reported in the Montreal *Gazette* on 22 January, no visit took place. The Wallis Gimson & Co. plates are not commemorative of a Canadian event, although they do carry a potter's view of Canada.

All the Canadian views included in "The World" pattern were based on photographs, as were probably all the other views (English, European, American) in the series. Who took or published the Canadian photographs has not been established. In the 1880s scenes such as appeared in this pattern proliferated, many of them as stereographs.

Though Wallis Gimson & Co. went out of business in 1890, Canadian china merchants would have had supplies of their wares on hand for a while longer. Goods ordered at the end of the 1880s might not be sold out for several years. There is at least one record of "The World" earthenware being given as a Canadian wedding present in 1892. On 7 March that year Isabella Ross, daughter of William Ross of St Malachie d'Ormstown in Chateauguay County, Quebec, married David Pringle of Huntingdon County. They set up housekeeping on Pringle's farm, "Winton Hill," where their wedding presents were put to daily use. A meat dish printed with the views of Notre Dame church in Montreal and the Parliament Buildings in Ottawa survived hard use and is now in the possession of their granddaughter, Mrs William Tetley of Montreal.[15]

During the later years of the nineteenth century some British potters produced earthenware printed not with views of Canada but with portraits of eminent persons associated with the Dominion. A pair of octagonal plates, printed usually in black but sometimes in brown, with portraits of Sir John A. Macdonald, first prime minister of the Dominion of Canada, and the Hon. Edward Blake, leader of the federal Liberal party and Macdonald's unsuccessful political opponent from 1879 to 1887, belong to the 1880s. They have no maker's mark, but the photographs from which the portraits were copied were taken by William James Topley of Ottawa. The Macdonald portrait was reproduced in many publications. The Marquis of Lorne (governor-general of Canada from 1878 to 1883) had a personal copy of it and used it as an illustration in his *Canadian Pictures*, published in 1884. It was the frontispiece to volume II of Joseph Pope's *Memoirs of the Right Hon. Sir John Alexander Macdonald*, published in 1894.

The Macdonald and Blake plates, although unidentified as to maker, would seem to have been from the same anonymous British pottery that produced a series of similarly shaped and designed portrait plates commemorating royalty and public figures in Great Britain. A dated plate in the series recorded the 1886 opening of an English hospital by Prince Albert Victor, elder son of the Prince of Wales. Roses, shamrocks, and thistles surround the portraits of the overseas personages, maple leaves the Canadians. The Canadian coat of arms, as it was in the 1880s, is printed above Macdonald and Blake. In this series, the portraits are always identified on the face of the plate. Gilding was usually added around the rim.

Commemorative items from British potteries had a long history of sales appeal in Canada. In 1851 Louisa Stacey, an immigrant living in Canada East (now the Province of Quebec), wrote to her grandfather in England that jugs issued to mark the Great Exhibition, held that year in London, were selling in Sherbrooke. The latest things "seem to reach us from England so much quicker than they used to," she added, "now that the steam ships are running."[16]

A commemorative jug that appeared on the market some twenty years after Louisa Stacey noted items of this type on sale in the Eastern Townships became associated with Canada, although it had not originally been produced because of any Canadian connection. Issued in honour of the 1871 marriage of Queen Victoria's fourth daughter, the Princess Louise, to the Marquis of Lorne, son of the Duke of Argyll, the jug carried the portraits of the young couple printed in purple and surrounded by wreaths of English roses and Scottish thistles. When the Marquis of Lorne was appointed governor-general of Canada a few years later there must have been added interest in this item commemorative not only of a marriage in which Scots everywhere took pride but of a governor-general who was to make a lasting impression on the cultural life of the country. With the Princess Louise, Lord Lorne founded the Royal Canadian Academy of Arts in 1880; in 1882 he founded the Royal Society of Canada. Sir William Dawson, first president of the Royal Society, spoke of Lord Lorne as a governor-general who identified himself with "the higher intellectual life of the Dominion" more fully than any of his predecessors in the vice-regal office.[17] He was to be remembered as "the patron of progress and culture."

That the Lorne and Louise jugs would have had a sale in Canada was virtually assured on two counts: the number of Scots in Canada (by the 1870s they were half a million strong), and by the fact the jugs were products of a Scottish pottery long associated with the Canadian market. Although many of these jugs are unmarked, the example in the collections of the National Museum of Man carries the maker's name, COCHRAN, printed on the bottom (Figure 23). The jugs were, therefore, from the same Glasgow pottery that had earlier sent agents to Canada to gather in orders and which, in the 1880s, would be supplying Francis Thomas with his views of Quebec. Their popularity is borne out by the frequency with which they could be found, some years ago, in second-hand shops and at house auctions, particularly in country districts where Scottish immigrants had settled.

Testimony to the sales appeal of the subjects chosen by the earthenware potters for these commemorative plates and jugs comes from the porcelain makers. Princess Louise, the Marquis of Lorne, Edward Blake, and Sir John A. Macdonald (Plates 145, 146, 147, 148), were all available as busts or statuettes in the British-invented porcelain called Parian. Also in Parian was a bust of Hon. Alexander Mackenzie, who defeated Macdonald in the election of 1873 to become the first Liberal prime minister of Canada. (Mackenzie was ousted by Macdonald in the next election and it was then that Blake

FIGURE 23
Mark on commemorative jugs

took over as the leader of the federal Liberals.) "Sir John A." was so popular, in fact, that in 1886 a Toronto newspaper offered free terra cotta busts of him as an inducement for new subscriptions.[18]

In their enthusiasm for Canadian scenes on earthenware some collectors have included wares printed with animals indigenous to Canada. Unfortunately, many animals are native to more than one country. These include the moose, beaver, otter, and polar bear, all of which were featured, along with tropical and other animals, in a blue-printed multi-scene pattern entitled "Quadrupeds." The maker was the Staffordshire potter, John Hall, the date about 1825–30. Any animals in this series that may be considered Canadian could just as easily be identified with the United States or, in the case of the polar bear, for example, with countries such as Greenland. Hall set the animals against fragmentary landscapes (the beaver is posed against a formally conceived waterfall, the moose against conventionally jagged peaks). None of the glimpses of landscapes in Hall's scenes has as yet been identified as from any Canadian view.

Hall was not alone in producing an animal series. Enoch Wood & Sons were the makers of a blue-printed pattern which put the emphasis on hunting such animals as elephants, tigers, leopards, and (as with Hall's series) polar bears and moose. The polar bear scene, with a sailing ship that is probably a whaler in the background, bears a relation to, although it is not taken directly from, an engraving entitled "A View of the WHALE-FISHERY, and the manner of KILLING BEARS near & on the Coast of Greenland." This Greenland scene appeared as an illustration in Charles Theodore Middleton's *A New and Complete System of Geography*, published in London in 1779. It may have been taken from a travel book of the period which would have had other illustrations on the same theme. There is always the possibility that some of the Woods' animal scenes were based on scenes in Canada but until positive identification is made, they, like Hall's fragmentary views, must remain purely speculative. The date of the Woods' pattern is about the same as Hall's, but Enoch Wood & Sons did not give their pattern a name. To those who do collect it, it is generally known as a "zoological" series.

One of the greatest triumphs of the British potters was their mastery and commerical exploitation of underglaze transfer printing on earthenware. As the French potter, St Amans, said at the time of the Great Exhibition, the British led the world in the variety of their printed earthenware, available in "every tint." Of all the vast outpourings of printed patterns – in the unsurpassed blues, the sober greys and browns, the fresh greens, pinks, and mauves – none had a more enthusiastic reception than those which turned the dinner table into a picture gallery. The sublime, the romantic, the literal all had a place as the nineteenth century unfolded. Not only scenery, but people and events gave the potters scope for what the Canadian importers hailed each season as "CROCKERY ... a ... varied assortment."

PLATES

All photographs of earthenware from the collections of the National Museum of Man, National Museums of Canada, Ottawa, were taken by Harry Foster.

Photographs of documentary material were provided by the National Gallery of Canada, Ottawa (Plates 72, 131); the National Library of Canada, Ottawa (Plates 26, 29, 30, 34); the Public Archives of Canada, Ottawa (Plates 42, 59, 69); McCord Museum, McGill University, Montreal (Plates 4, 18, 38, 49, 51, 52); Cunard Line, Toronto (Plate 19); the British Library, London, England (Plate 8); the Public Record Office, Kew, England (Plates 56, 83); Geo. L. Ashworth & Bros Ltd, Hanley, England (Plates 62, 78); Josiah Wedgwood & Sons Ltd, Barlaston, England (Plates 1, 2).

Documentary material was also drawn from private collections and these photographs were taken by A. Kilbertus (Plates 13, 14, 31, 32, 66, 73, 90, 96, 97, 99, 100, 103, 109, 111, 113, 115, 123, 128, 134, 136).

PLATE 1

Engraving designs for "the much admired 'blue printed pots.'" From Enoch Wood & Sons'
booklet, 1827.

PLATE 2

A printer and transferrers at work. From *A Representation of the Manufacturing of Earthenware*
(1827).

The Death of Wolfe on a Wedgwood jug, c. 1780. Jugs with this decoration vary as to date, maker, and size. H. 22 cm.

PLATE 4

The Death of General Wolfe. Engraving by William Woollett after Benjamin West, published in
1776.

PLATE 5

Blue-printed platter, Jones & Son, 1820s. Strainers also have this version of Wolfe's death.
L. 51.7 cm.

PLATE 6
Enoch Wood & Sons' Pottery, Burslem, as it appeared at the time when Canadian scenes were being produced.

PLATE 7
"Table Rock, Niagara" on Enoch Wood & Sons soup plate printed in dark blue and in date 1830–40. Dia. 26 cm.

PLATE 8
Paul Svinin's view of Table Rock published in 1818 in *A Picturesque Voyage in North America.*

PLATE 9
"Fall of Montmorenci near Quebec," Enoch Wood & Sons. Note General Haldimand's summer
house. Dia. 22.9 cm.

PLATE 10
"Quebec" on interior of Enoch Wood & Sons vegetable dish with typical shell border, 1830–40.
W. 21.2 cm.

PLATE 11
The vegetable dish of Plate 10 complete with its cover. Scenes on the cover are American, not
Canadian.

PLATE 12
Rare egg hoop (open-ended egg cup) shows early St Lawrence steamboat (buildings on the reverse). H. 4 cm.

PLATE 13
This Montreal view engraved by W.S. Leney and published in 1830 by Adolphus Bourne inspired two potters. See Plates 15 and 17.

PLATE 14
Detail from Montreal harbour view published by Bourne. Potters took the canoe from this
scene (Plates 15, 17).

PLATE 15
Davenport stand, pierced rim, "Montreal" pattern (based on the engravings in Plates 13
and 14), c. 1835. L. 25 cm.

PLATE 16
The stand in Plate 15 with its matching fruit basket. These items are rare in Davenport's "Montreal."

PLATE 17
One of the rarest Canadian views is this version of Montreal on a tureen stand. Unmarked,
1835–40. L. 22 cm.

PLATE 18
Detail from Robert Sproule's original water-colour published by Bourne as an engraving in
1830.

PLATE 19
Sir Samuel Cunard (1787–1865), the Novascotian whose steamships were popular
decoration on pottery.

PLATE 20
Sauce boat, "Acadia" pattern named for one of Cunard's first steamships. Printed in mulberry.
L. 19.3 cm.

PLATE 21

Plate, Edwards, printed in black with a view of the Ladies' Cabin ("Boston Mails" pattern).
Dia. 26.4 cm.

PLATE 22

Shell dish, Edwards, showing the Gentlemen's Cabin. The number of figures may vary in this
view. L. 23 cm.

PLATE 23

Plate, Edwards, printed in lavender. The title is often omitted on these small items. Note border. Dia. 9.4 cm.

PLATE 24

Platter, Edwards, with the 1841 registry mark on the back. Another view of the Gentlemen's
Cabin. L. 35 cm.

PLATE 24A

Blue-printed platter, Edwards, view of Ladies' Cabin with full border, L. 38 cm.

PLATE 25
Blue-printed plate, "Arctic Scenery" pattern. Compare border variations in Plates 27 and 28.
Dia. 27 cm.

PLATE 26
Part of this 1824 engraving from Parry's *Journal of a Second Voyage* was used in "Arctic Scenery"
(Plate 25).

PLATE 27
"Arctic Scenery" platter. The shooting man is taken from an engraving in Parry's 1824 *Journal*.
L. 43 cm.

PLATE 28

"Arctic Scenery" soup plate. See Plates 29, 30, 31 for elements of the design (view and border).
Dia. 26.7 cm.

PLATE 29

Sledges of the Esquimaux appeared in Parry's *Journal of a Second Voyage* and was adapted for
pottery use.

PLATE 30

Parry's *Hecla* and *Griper* in winter harbour, from his 1821 *Journal.* They later appeared on tableware (Plate 28).

PLATE 31

This African lion, from a volume published in 1834, helps to date "Arctic Scenery" (see Plate 28).

PLATE 32
W.H. Bartlett (1809–54), whose popular Canadian views were seized on by Staffordshire potters.

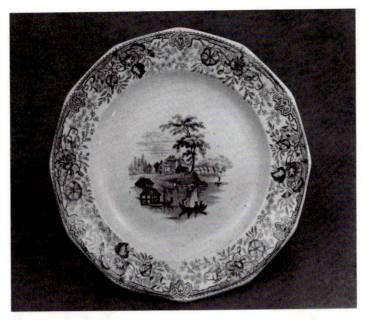

PLATE 33
Plate, T. Godwin, brown-printed with a view taken from Bartlett's Village of Cedars (Plate 66). Dia. 18 cm.

JOHN McDONALD.

BEGS LEAVE TO ACQUAINT HIS FRIENDS and the public in TOWN and COUNTRY, that he has received by the Helena and Father Mathew from Liverpool his Fall Supply of

CHINA AND EARTHENWARE,

Consisting of GOLD Burnished and other China Tea and Breakfast Sets, with Plates to match, a few choice Dinner Sets of FANCY and Wilton Patterns ogether with Patterns of do. with British North American Views, which can be got to order; China and Lustre ware Oranments, MUGS, JUGS, Toilet Sets, &c. &c. which together with his present Stock of GLASSWARE, consisting of Decanters, Wines, Tumblers, Preserve Plates and Dishes, will be sold at the lowest prices for CASH.

Orders from the Country attended to, as usual, with punctuality and despatch.

January 26.

PLATE 34
This Halifax advertisement ran for two years, from the end of 1843. Note "British North American Views."

PLATE 35
Blue-printed ewer, Podmore, Walker & Co.'s "British America" pattern (Quebec). See Plate 36.
H. 27 cm.

PLATE 36
Basin to match the ewer in Plate 35. The view is Bartlett's Quebec, from the opposite shore.
Dia. 34 cm.

PLATE 37
Blue-printed well-and-tree platter, "British America" pattern, with a view of Montreal.
L. 54.4 cm.

PLATE 38
Bartlett's Montreal (from the St Lawrence) published in *Canadian Scenery*.
See Plate 37.

PLATE 39
Blue-printed dish with moulded rim design, Podmore, Walker & Co. The view is Port Hope.
W. 27.5 cm.

PLATE 40
Platter, Podmore, Walker & Co.'s "British America" pattern. View is of Kingston, Lake Ontario.
L. 40.2 cm.

PLATE 41

Plate printed in blue with the central portion of Bartlett's View from the Citadel at Kingston.
Dia. 19 cm.

PLATE 42

Bartlett's Kingston, Lake Ontario, a view used by Podmore, Walker & Co.
See Plate 40.

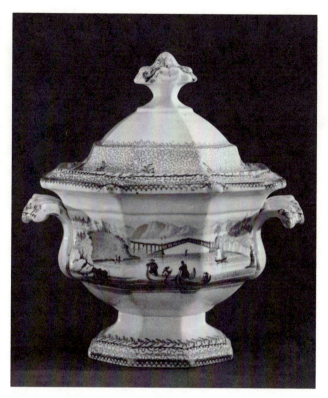

PLATE 43
Sauce tureen. Podmore, Walker & Co.'s version of Bartlett's Chaudière Bridge, with canoes
added. H. 19 cm.

PLATE 44
Tureen stand. Adapted view of Navy Island, a Bartlett scene used more literally on plates.
Dia. 11.5 cm.

PLATE 45
Plate, Podmore, Walker & Co., Indian Scene. The mark on the back includes PEARL STONE
WARE. Dia. 24.4 cm.

PLATE 46
Bartlett's Indian Scene. See Plate 45 and note how the scene was reduced to fit the space on
earthenware.

PLATE 47
Covered dish, Podmore, Walker & Co. Different Bartlett views are on the cover and interior.
H. 21.1 cm.

PLATE 48
The Governor's House, Fredericton on the dish in Plate 47. The Chaudière Bridge is on the cover. W. 25.2 cm.

PLATE 49
Bartlett's The Governor's House, Fredericton. The view was offered on pottery in a choice of colours.

PLATE 50
Plate, Podmore, Walker & Co., with detail (church, buildings) from St Regis, Indian Village.
Dia. 13.3 cm.

PLATE 51
Detail from Bartlett's St Regis, Indian Village used in multi-scene "British America" pattern.

PLATE 52
Bartlett's Outlet of Lake Memphremagog, a view that appeared on a variety of ceramic wares.

PLATE 53
Covered dish, Ridgway, Morley, Wear & Co., with a Canadian scene (Plate 52) on the interior.
H. 15.8 cm.

PLATE 54
Interior of dish in Plate 53. The view is from Plate 52 with details from other Bartlett scenes.
W. 25 cm.

PLATE 55
Soup tureen, cover, stand. Morley's 1845 registry mark is on the tureen. The view is from
Plate 52. H. 27 cm.

PLATE 56
Morley's "dinner service" shape, as entered in the Register of Designs, 31 May 1845. See
Plates 55, 57.

PLATE 57
Vegetable dish cover (Sir William Dawson's service) printed in grey on the shape seen in
Plate 56.

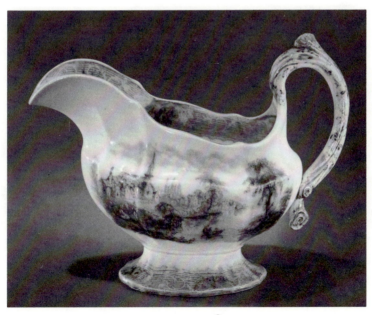

PLATE 58
Sauce boat has registry mark. Bartlett's Village of Cedars. Georgeville is found on its stand.
L. 17.5 cm.

PLATE 59

Bartlett's Chaudière Bridge near Quebec. See Plates 43, 60. It appears also on the cover in Plate 47.

PLATE 60

Plate in Morley's multi-scene "Lake" pattern. The scene is the Chaudière Bridge (Plate 59). Dia. 26 cm.

PLATE 57
Vegetable dish cover (Sir William Dawson's service) printed in grey on the shape seen in
Plate 56.

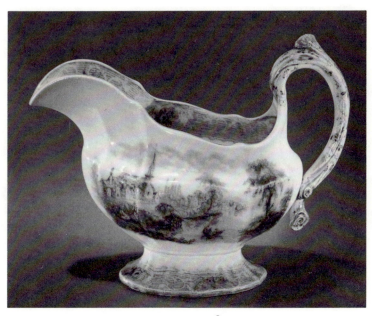

PLATE 58
Sauce boat has registry mark. Bartlett's Village of Cedars. Georgeville is found on its stand.
L. 17.5 cm.

PLATE 59

Bartlett's Chaudière Bridge near Quebec. See Plates 43, 60. It appears also on the cover in Plate 47.

PLATE 60

Plate in Morley's multi-scene "Lake" pattern. The scene is the Chaudière Bridge (Plate 59). Dia. 26 cm.

PLATE 61

Morley jug printed with Bartlett's Kingston, Lake Ontario. The pottery engraver added trees.
H. 27 cm.

PLATE 62

Pull from an old copperplate used by Ashworth & Bros (Morley's successors). Compare
Plates 45 and 46.

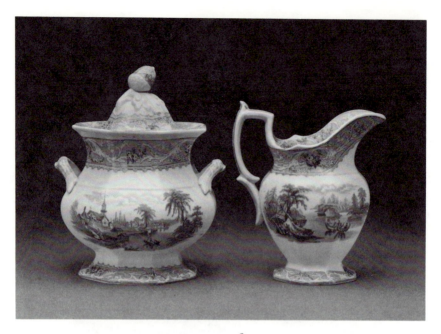

PLATE 63

Teaware. Note acorn knob. Plates sometimes have moulded acorns and leaves around the rim.
H. of jug 14.7 cm.

PLATE 64

Three views (Plates 62, 66, 80) decorate this Morley blue-printed sauce tureen, cover and stand.
H. 17 cm.

PLATE 65
Tureen, Podmore, Walker & Co. The wayside cross (left) is retained in this Village of Cedars.
H. 10.5 cm.

PLATE 66
Bartlett's Village of Cedars. Compare the potters' versions in Plates 33, 63, 64, and 65.

PLATE 67
Morley platter. This scene was used on articles as varied as soup tureens and vases
(Plates 55, 79). L. 38.5 cm.

PLATE 68
Black-printed Morley plate. View of the Rideau Canal, Bytown (in the heart of modern
Ottawa). Dia. 23.7 cm.

PLATE 69

Bartlett's Rideau Canal, Bytown used by Morley (Plate 68). His successors also offered it in blue or brown.

PLATE 70

Platter, "Lake" pattern, printed in grey. The scene is Bartlett's Hallowell.

L. 49.2 cm.

PLATE 71
Morley plate, blue-printed with Scene among the Thousand Isles (see Plates 72, 73).
Dia. 23 cm.

PLATE 72
Bartlett's original drawing of the Scene among the Thousand Isles. Brown wash heightened
with white.

PLATE 73
The published steel engraving followed Bartlett's drawing closely. The pottery engraver made
changes.

PLATE 74
Blue-printed "Lake" teapot. Georgeville. "Lake" teapots occur also in other shapes.
H. 22 cm.

PLATE 75
Light blue "Lake" plate. Bartlett's Church at Point Levi. Found occasionally in purple.
Dia. 20 cm.

PLATE 76
"Lake" toilet ware, the basin with an interpolated view. The ewer has an importers' mark in date
1858–62.

PLATE 77
"Lake" platter, interpolated scene in green. Probably of the Morley & Ashworth period.
L. 43.8 cm.

PLATE 78
Pull from a copperplate used by Ashworth & Bros who continued Morley's "Lake," using the
same border design.

PLATE 79
Green-printed Ashworth vases, ivory body. Outlet of Lake Memphremagog. Vases are rare.
H. 25.8 cm.

PLATE 80
Stand for tureen, Plate 64. Georgeville also appears on tea bowls, custard cups, jugs,
chamber pots. L. 21 cm.

PLATE 81
Soup tureen, cover, stand printed with Canadian symbols on Walley's registered shape
(Plate 82). H. 20 cm.

PLATE 82
Page from the Register of Designs, British Patent Office, shows Walley's "dinner set" shapes,
29 Nov. 1856.

PLATE 83
Wash basin printed in grey, maple leaves and beavers, with gilding top and bottom. Walley.
Dia. 34.5 cm.

PLATE 84
Walley cake plate has enamel bands and gilding but sometimes a printed floral border was used.
W. 25.5 cm.

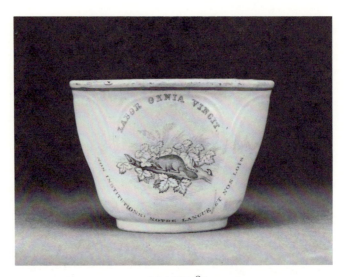

PLATE 85
Walley bowl. The reverse has the grey-printed maple leaves and beaver but no slogans.
H 11.4 cm.

PLATE 86
Brown-printed teaware. Furnival & Sons' pattern was also offered in multi-colour.
H. of jug 12.5 cm.

PLATE 87

T. Furnival & Sons registered this "shape for vegetable dish" on 20 Sept. 1884. Pattern is
"Maple." L. 29 cm.

PLATE 88

Blue-printed "Maple" plate, a fairly rare colour in this pattern made also in pink or green.
Dia. 21 cm.

PLATE 89

Ladles, Furnival & Sons' "Maple" pattern. The beaver was often omitted on small articles.
L. 26 cm.

PLATE 91

Black-printed plate from J. Marshall & Co., Bo'ness. The view is seen on the card in Plate 90.
Dia. 18 cm.

A prosperous New Year.

PLATE 90
This 1882 greeting card was published by Bennet & Co., Montreal. The same view appeared on pottery.

PLATE 92
Marshall & Co. called their pattern "Canadian Sports." A card with this view probably exists.
Dia. 19.1 cm.

PLATE 93
Black-printed "Canadian Sports" plate has JOHN MARSHALL & CO BO'NESS POTTERY impressed
mark. Dia. 18 cm.

PLATE 94
Blue-printed "Canadian Sports" jug. The scene in Plate 99 is on the reverse. See also Plate 96.
H. 24.5 cm.

PLATE 95
This plate in Marshall & Co.'s multi-scene pattern has an impressed makers' mark. See Plate 97.
Dia. 19 cm.

PLATE 96
One of a series of cards lithographed in colour and published by Bennet & Co., Montreal, in 1882. See Plate 94.

PLATE 97
The scene on this silk-fringed double card (see Plate 99 for reverse) appeared on plates, jugs, platters.

PLATE 98

Detail taken from the "Canadian Sports" basin in Plate 101. See Plate 99 for the source of the view.

PLATE 99
Silk-fringed double card (see Plate 97). The view seen here was reproduced on basins, plates, cups.

PLATE 100
This Bennet & Co. card was received by a Quebecker in 1882. The scene appears on the ewer in Plate 101.

PLATE 101

Ewer and basin, printed scenes with colours added. The basin has the impressed BO'NESS
POTTERY mark.

PLATE 102

Brown-printed ewer with colours added and pattern name on the bottom. Three views decorate it. H. 31 cm.

PLATE 103

The Canadian sports scene on this Bennet & Co. card appears on the front of the ewer in Plate 102.

PLATE 104
"Canadian Sports" plate with moulded border design and brown-printed snowshoeing scene.
Dia. 16.7 cm.

PLATE 105
Black-printed "Canadian Sports" plate with the usual printed border and a lacrosse scene.
Dia. 17 cm.

PLATE 106
Detail from the basin in Plate 101. In Victorian days lacrosse was Canada's national sport.

PLATE 107
Jug, "Canadian Sports" pattern name on bottom but interpolated scene. Traces of
gilding. H. 21.8 cm.

PLATE 108
Brown-printed plate, multi-scene "Quebec" pattern made in Glasgow for a Quebec importer.
Dia. 25.6 cm.

PLATE 109
View adapted to pottery use (Plate 108) helps date "Quebec" pattern. Dufferin Terrace was
opened in 1879.

PLATE 110

Pink-printed soup plate with a view of the St Louis Gate. Most views had bilingual titles.
Dia. 24.1 cm.

PLATE 111

This view of Quebec's St Louis Gate was obviously the source for the pottery decoration in
Plate 110.

PLATE 112
Platter, marked Britannia Pottery, Glasgow. Plate 113 shows the source of the view.
L. 28.2 cm.

PLATE 113
St John's Gate, Vallée photograph published by Holiwell with the same bilingual title as on
Plate 112.

PLATE 114

Pink-printed platter with name of Quebec importer, F.T. Thomas, on the back. See Plate 115. L. 46 cm.

QUEBEC, HARBOUR. & LEVIS

HÂVRE DE QUÉBEC & LEVIS

PLATE 115

Quebec Harbour & Levis. See Plate 114 and note clouds added by pottery engraver to fill white space.

PLATE 116
Soup tureen cover has view of Quebec from Point Levis (another of the views published by Holiwell).

PLATE 117
Platter. This View Looking North from the Citadel was also used on an oval shape.
L. 34.2 cm.

PLATE 118

Wolfe's Monument, as Holiwell published it. Late plates may be marked FLEMING OF GLASGOW.
Dia. 18.4 cm.

PLATE 119

Three-piece soap dish, Wolfe & Montcalm Monument on cover, beaver border around dish.
Dia. 18.4 cm.

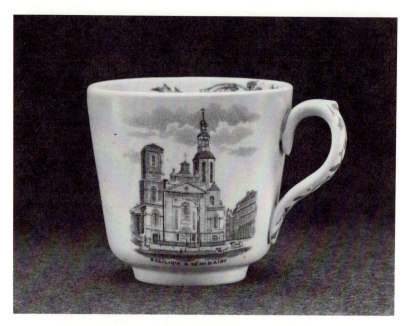

PLATE 120
Cup. Basilique & Séminaire on one side, Breakneck Steps on the other, border on the inside.
H. 7 cm.

PLATE 121
Basin accompanying the ewer in Plate 122 has Chaudière Falls on the inside and border
repeated outside.

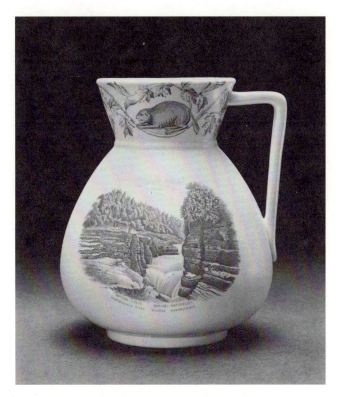

PLATE 122

Ewer goes with basin in Plate 121 and has view in Plate 123. The shape was popular in the 1890s. H. 25.9 cm.

NATURAL STEPS.
MONTMORENCY RIVER.

MARCHES NATURELLES.
RIVIERE MONTMORENCY

PLATE 123

Natural Steps, Montmorency River, the view in Plate 122, as Holiwell published it with bilingual title.

PLATE 124
Covered dish, brown-printed with views of Cape Diamond, a different view on interior
(Plate 125).

PLATE 125
Lorette Falls on interior of dish in Plate 124. Late mark, B.P. Co. Ltd, printed in green.
L. 27.5 cm.

PLATE 126
Sugar bowl, view of Lorette Falls. Narrow border on bowl matches jug in Plate 130. Lid has usual border.

PLATE 127
Plate with view of Montmorency Fall and
abbreviated title. See Plate 128 for view's
source. Dia. 14 cm.

PLATE 128
Holiwell's title for the view in Plate 127 was
Montmorency Fall, Summer View. The
potter shortened it.

PLATE 129
Small plate with Montmorency Fall, Winter View. Here the potter omitted the French title.
Dia. 14 cm.

PLATE 130
Jug with narrow border seen in Plates 119, 126. Source was Vallée stereograph. See Plate 131.
H. 13.3 cm.

PLATE 131
Vallée stereograph (right side), titled unilingually on the back Abraham Hill. The source for
Plate 130.

PLATE 132
Butter pad (nineteenth-century term for these small articles). View is Breakneck Steps.
Dia. 7.3 cm.

PLATE 133
Cup. Seated figure is untitled on earthenware but see Plate 134 for identification.
H. 7 cm.

PLATE 135
Cup with untitled figure in front, other views on sides, and border inside. See Plate 136.
H. 7 cm.

PLATE 134
Holiwell's title was Lorette Squaw. Indians at Lorette (near Quebec City) were of the Huron tribe.

PLATE 136
Holiwell, whose published views were based on Vallée photographs, called this figure Indian Chief.

PLATE 137
Plate, dark blue, view of Quebec. Probably early 1830s. View's source may have been Plate 138.
Dia. 23 cm.

PLATE 138
Detail from A General View of Quebec from Point Levy, published in 1761. Compare with
Plate 137.

PLATE 139
Platter. Though with a building faintly resembling Dundurn, Hamilton, this view is fanciful.
L. 48.7 cm.

PLATE 140
Brown-printed teaware, "Ontario Lake Scenery." Typical Victorian fanciful view.
H., tea bowl, 7.9 cm.

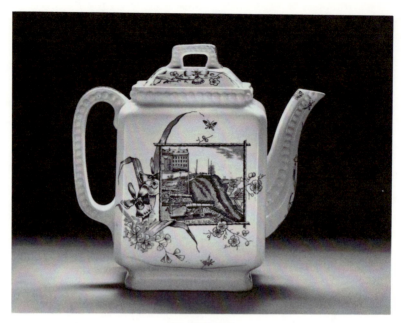

PLATE 141
Teapot, "The World" pattern. Grand Battery, Quebec; Normal School, Toronto on reverse.
H. 20.3 cm.

PLATE 142
Platter in "The World" pattern (registered 27 May 1884). Ottawa and Montreal views.
L. 39.3 cm.

PLATE 143
Brown-printed saucer, Normal School, Toronto. Sometimes flowers are in colours.
Dia. 16.5 cm.

PLATE 144
Green-printed platter, traces of gilding. Niagara views. Sometimes in two-colour printing.
L. 45.3 cm.

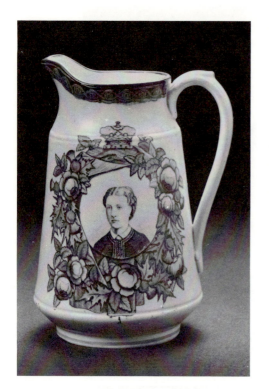 

PLATES 145 and 146
Jug, 1870s. Princess Louise and Marquis of Lorne. COCHRAN mark. Similar commemorative
items came from other potters. H. 20.2 cm.

PLATE 147
Black-printed plate of the 1880s with gilding on the rim. Portrait of Edward Blake.
Dia. 24.5 cm.

PLATE 148
First prime minister of the Dominion of Canada. Sir John A. Macdonald, from a photograph by
W.J. Topley.

GLOSSARY

The following is a brief glossary of some of the ceramic terms used in the text. A number of ceramic terms have more than one meaning. The explanations given here refer to the use of these terms in the context of this work.

Black Basaltes

Fine black stoneware. In the 1760s Josiah Wedgwood began experiments to obtain a refinement of a traditional Staffordshire body known as "black Egyptian." For his ware he chose the name black basaltes. Others making a dry-bodied ware of similar type began using Wedgwood's name for it. Today all these wares are generally spoken of as basaltes, but Canadian importers of the eighteenth and early nineteenth centuries tended to use the old name. George Pozer of Quebec, for example, ordered "Black Egyptian Tea Pots ... of the neatest & newest patterns" to be sent out from London with the first spring shipments of 1787.

China

Strictly speaking, china implies porcelain, but the term has long been used loosely, as in "china collectors" (collectors whose interests may include any form of ceramic wares). When Canadian importers of the early days (such as George Pozer) used the word "china" in their orders or advertisements, they almost always meant porcelain. A "china merchant," however, meant a seller of ceramic wares in general. Early china merchants in Canada dealt in a variety of goods, many of them completely unrelated to ceramic wares.

Creamware

Lead-glazed earthenware whose appearance might range from a very light to a very deep cream. When one of the Hessian officers serving with British troops near Quebec City in 1776 noted that French-Canadian farmers had "tea services of English yellow-ware," he was describing cream-coloured earthenware. In Canadian advertisements it was also referred to as "cream-coloured," "C. C.," and "queensware." See **Queensware**.

Crockery

Sellers of Victorian wares in Canada often referred to their ceramic stock as "crockery." It was a term more apt to be used by the general merchant than the specialist dealer, although Canadian china merchants did sometimes refer to themselves as "crockery sellers."

Earthenware

The earthenwares on which Canadian views were printed were wares that burned white in the kiln. All earthenwares, when fired, are opaque; they are also porous until glazed.

Edged wares

As used in Canadian advertisements, "edged wares" usually meant earthenware with a slightly moulded rim design, the moulding "varnished" (i.e., painted) over in blue or green, etc. George Pozer ordered "blew edg'd" plates to be sent to him in Quebec from Liverpool in 1798. By Victorian times edged wares had moved into the category of "common wares," described in advertisements as "suitable for the country trade."

Granite china

See **Ironstone china**. Ridgway, Morley, Wear & Co. used a granite china body for their "Agricultural Vase" pattern.

Ironstone china

Not a china (i.e., porcelain) but a high-fired, dense earthenware, strong and durable. The name was patented in 1813 by the Staffordshire potter Charles James Mason but, as with Wedgwood's Queensware, the name was borrowed by others and became a generic term. What was essentially the same body was made by many potters using a score or more of

different names for it, such as granite china, stone china, etc. J. & T. Edwards, who registered the "Boston Mails" pattern in 1841, printed some of it on a body with the impressed mark IRONSTONE CHINA.

Multi-scene

In this type of pattern different views or subjects decorate the various articles of a table service (one view on soup plates, another on tureens, and so on). Simeon Shaw, in his *History of the Staffordshire Potteries* (1829), described multi-scene patterns: "a certain ornamental border is employed for all the plates whatever be their size; but every plate [i.e., each size] has a different Landscape ..." Most of the potters' views of Canada were multi-scene patterns.

Opaque china

Another name for a durable earthenware of the ironstone type. Thomas Godwin printed his Canadian views on a body marked OPAQUE CHINA.

Parian

A type of English porcelain originally intended to simulate marble. It went by various names, including "statuary porcelain," but Herbert Minton's name, Parian (after marble from the Greek island of Paros), eventually prevailed. First made in the 1840s, its popularity continued for the rest of the century. Busts of famous Canadians, including Sir John A. Macdonald, were made in Parian.

Pearl stone

Still another name for an ironstone-type body. Podmore, Walker & Co. used the name PEARL STONE WARE for the body on which they printed their Canadian views.

Pearl ware

As distinct from "pearl stone ware" (a

nineteenth-century ironstone-type ware), pearl ware was an earthenware much the same as creamware but whiter in appearance. Josiah Wedgwood introduced a "pearl" earthenware in the eighteenth century but made little of it. The name occurs occasionally in Canadian advertisements of the very early nineteenth century. Most of the Canadian views were printed on an earthenware body that provided a white background for the printing.

Porcelain

Porcelain, unlike earthenware, is usually translucent, but the translucency test is not infallible. The potters' views of Canada considered in this book were printed on earthenware, not porcelain, bodies.

Porcelaine à la perle

This was not a porcelain at all but a name used by James Edwards (who carried on the "Boston Mails" pattern) for an ironstone-type earthenware. In the second half of the nineteenth century British earthenware makers found their markets being eroded by the makers of inexpensive French porcelain, and adopting French-sounding names for their ironstone-type bodies and giving these bodies the faintly grey look of continental porcelain was one way of meeting the competition.

Pottery

Earthenware.

Pratt ware

Earthenware of late eighteenth- and early nineteenth-century date with decoration in a distinctive palette (the high temperature colours include yellow, orange, green, and a dull blue). The name Pratt is associated with them because some of the wares are marked PRATT, but most are unmarked and they obviously originated at a number of different potteries. Pratt-type plaques moulded in low relief with the death of Wolfe occur.

Queensware

Josiah Wedgwood adopted this name for his perfected creamware body after he had received royal patronage for it in the 1760s. Others quickly helped themselves to the name, so that Canadian advertisements, such as the one in the *Royal Gazette and New Brunswick Advertiser* on 1 September 1795 for "Queen's Ware," do not necessarily imply a Wedgwood product.

Semi-china

Another name for an earthenware body. Enoch Wood & Sons used a "semi-china" body for their Canadian views.

Stone china

See **Ironstone china**.

Stoneware

Any stonewares mentioned in this text would be of the fine-grained, dry-bodied type. Samuel Hollins, a Staffordshire potter, used a buff stoneware for relief-moulded jugs depicting the Death of Wolfe. Stoneware might be of various colours, such as the "Red Tea Pots" and "Buff Colour'd" jugs George Pozer was ordering from Quebec in 1787. Wares of this type are non-porous when fired.

Terra cotta

Unglazed earthenware usually taken to have burned red in the kiln (a terra cotta shade), but the colour could vary considerably, and some terra cotta ornaments were very light in colour. In 1886 a Toronto newspaper was giving away terra cotta busts of Sir John A. Macdonald. Although normally unglazed, terra cotta wares could be glazed and decorated in enamel colours.

Transfer printing

See Chapter 1. A succinct description was given in the *Art Union* in 1844: "Engravings are transferred from copperplates to porcelain and earthenware through the intervention of paper, on which the impressions are first made ..."

NOTES

INTRODUCTION

1 Alfred Hawkins, *Picture of Quebec* (Quebec 1834), 7.

2 [S.C. Hall], "The Potteries," *Art Union* (May 1844), 134.

3 J.E. Cabot, "On the Relation of Art to Nature," *Atlantic Monthly* (Feb. 1864), 191.

4 R.W. Binns, *A Century of Potting in the City of Worcester* (Worcester 1865), 55.

5 [S.C. Hall], "The Potteries," 134.

1 PRINTING ON POTTERY

1 A nineteenth-century British employer (a cotton printer named Thomas) described the British workman in these terms. He is quoted in W.J. Reader, *Life in Victorian England* (London 1964), 1.

2 Faujas de St Fond, quoted in E.A. Sandeman, *Notes on the Manufacture of Earthenware* (London 1921), 6.

3 M. de St Amans, quoted in *The Crystal Palace and Its Contents ... An Illustrated Cyclopaedia of the Great Exhibition ...* (London 1852), 214. St Amans had spent time in England and was acquainted with Staffordshire methods before he became involved with the French potting industry at Montereau. See W.P. Jervis, *The Encyclopedia of Ceramics* (New York 1902), 395, 508.

4 *The Repository of Arts, Literature, Commerce, Manufactures, Fashions and Politics*, Feb. 1809, 107; April 1809, 330.

5 "A Day at the Staffordshire Potteries," *The Penny Magazine*, 27 May 1843, 207. Much of this article, published in London, was reproduced in *The Albion* (29 July 1843), a magazine published in New York in the British interest and with a large Canadian subscription list.

6 M. Digby Wyatt, *On the Influence Exercised on Ceramic Manufactures by the Late Mr. Herbert Minton* (London 1858), 6. This was a paper read before the Society of Arts on 26 May 1858, and later privately published by Wyatt.

7 Dionysius Lardner, ed., *Treatise on the*

Origin, Progressive Improvement and Present State of the Manufacture of Porcelain and Glass (London 1832), 96–7.

8 The process may have been used briefly in Italy at the Doccia factory prior to its use in England. See Robert Copeland, *Spode's Willow Pattern & Other Designs after the Chinese* (London 1980), 30 n. vii.

9 P. Angers, *Les Seigneurs et premiers censitaires de St-Georges-Beauce et la famille Pozer* (Beauceville 1927), 19–25; William Henderson to Sir James M. LeMoine, 5 Jan. 1869, in LeMoine, *Maple Leaves*, series VII (Quebec 1906), 287; Benjamin Sulte, "Le Chien d'Or," *Le Bulletin des recherches historiques*, Sept. 1915, 270; Elizabeth Collard, "Orders of a Quebec China Merchant," *Canadian Collector*, July–Aug. 1976, 32–5.

10 This letter and order are with the Pozer papers in the McCord Museum of McGill University. The order is for "Blue printed," the normal way in which Canadian china merchants referred to earthenware with underglaze blue printing. When porcelain was meant, the word "china" was generally used; an examination of Pozer's surviving orders shows he followed the common practice.

11 Frobisher Papers, McLennan Library, McGill University. Frobisher died later that year and Shuter submitted the bill to his executors.

12 *Royal Gazette* (Halifax), 13 March 1811.

13 William Evans, *Art and History of the Potting Business, Compiled from the Most Practical Sources, for the Especial Use of Working Potters* (Shelton 1846), 37.

14 *New Brunswick Courier* (Saint John), 28 June 1834.

15 *Missiskoui Standard* (Frelighsburg), 2 June 1835.

16 *Bytown Gazette*, 10 Nov. 1836.

17 Wyatt, *Influence ... on Manufactures*, 28.

18 *Illustrated London News*, 26 July 1851.

19 Alexander Christie's advertisement in the *Niagara Chronicle*, 26 July 1851.

20 Hippolyte Taine, quoted in Arthur Bryant, *English Saga* (London 1941), 153.

21 Canniff Haight, "Ontario Fifty Years Ago and Now," *Canadian Monthly and National Review*, May 1881, 453.

22 J.T.S. Lidstone, *The Thirteenth Londoniad ...* (The Potteries 1866), 108. Lidstone was a doggerel versifier but his account of a visit to the Staffordshire potteries is valuable historically.

23 *Journal* (St Catharines), 12 Oct. 1831.

24 *Edmonton Bulletin*, 27 June 1895.

2 THE DEATH OF WOLFE

1 C. Reginald Grundy, "British Military and Naval Prints," *Connoisseur*, Oct. 1914, 72.

2 For an illustration of these two figures see Bernard Rackham, *Catalogue of the Schreiber Collection* (London 1915), I, pl. 4.

3 For illustrations of these Worcester items see Cyril Cook, *The Life and Work of Robert Hancock* (London 1948), pls. 15, 66, 120.

4 From John Galt's *Life ... and Studies of Benjamin West* (1820), quoted in Edgar Andrew Collard, "Benjamin West," *Gazette* (Montreal), 24 March 1951.

5 For a discussion of the identification of the figures in the central group in West's painting see J. Clarence Webster, *Wolfe and the Artists* (Toronto 1930), 64–9. See also Arthur Doughty and G.W. Parmelee, *The Siege of Quebec and the Battle of the Plains of Abraham* (Quebec 1901), III: 221–5; Régis Roy, "The Death of the Great Wolfe par West," *Le Bulletin des recherches historiques*, Jan. 1923, 30–1.

6 John Knox, who was present at the taking of Quebec, quoted in Doughty and Parmelee, *The Siege of Quebec*, 217.

7 Quoted in Doughty and Parmelee, ibid., 219.

8 Mrs Lynn Miller, Information Officer,

Wedgwood Museum, to author, 26 April 1982. It should be noted that on-glaze printing sometimes sinks into the glaze to such an extent that it may appear to be underglaze.

9 J.R. Kidson and Frank Kidson, *Historical Notices of the Leeds Old Pottery* (Leeds 1893), 72.

10 E.N. Stretton, "Thomas Rothwell, Engraver," *Antique Collector*, Oct.–Nov. 1971, 201–4.

11 William Turner, *Transfer Printing on Enamels, Porcelain and Pottery* (London 1907) 69–70, 134, and pl. B12.

12 For an illustration of one of these plaques see Roy Strong, *A Pageant of Canada* (Ottawa 1967), 178.

13 See chap. 1 for Pozer and Alport. Herculaneum's stoneware jugs are discussed in Alan Smith, "The Herculaneum China and Earthenware Manufactory," *English Ceramic Circle Transactions* 7, part 1 (1968): 32.

14 An example in the collections of the Royal Ontario Museum is illustrated in Brian Musselwhite, "'Death of Wolfe' on English Sugar Bowl," *Canadian Collector*, March–April 1978, 45.

15 Robert Wright, *The Life of Major-General James Wolfe Founded on Original Documents* (London 1864), 592.

16 "The Dinner-Table and Its Accessories," *Exhibition Supplement to The Illustrated London News*, 2 Aug. 1851.

17 The dates for the firm are suggested as c. 1826–8 in J.P. Cushion, *Pocket Book of British Ceramic Marks*, 3rd ed. (London 1976), 159.

3 CANADIAN SCENES FROM THE "FATHER OF THE POTTERIES"

1 *Staffordshire Advertiser*, 17 Dec. 1829, quoted in Frank Falkner, *The Wood Family of Burslem* (London 1912), 86.

2 Simeon Shaw, *History of the Staffordshire Potteries* (1829; reprint, London 1900), 30.

3 John Ward, *The Borough of Stoke-upon-Trent* (London 1843), 264.

4 *Montreal Gazette*, 29 Oct. 1829.

5 Pamela D. Kingsbury, "Enoch Wood Earthenware Found in St. Paul's Church, Burslem," *Antiques*, July 1977. (Reprinted in Paul Atterbury, ed., *English Pottery and Porcelain* [London 1980], 210–15.)

6 I am indebted to Arnold Mountford, Director of Museums, City of Stoke-on-Trent, Staffordshire, for checking the pieces for me. The contractor who demolished the church donated nearly 300 of the pieces found to the City Museum and Art Gallery, Stoke-on-Trent.

7 Shaw, *History of the Staffordshire Potteries*, 224.

8 [Annie Trumbull Slosson], *The China Hunters Club* (New York 1878), 159.

9 Alice Morse Earle, *China Collecting in America* (London 1892), 369–70.

10 W.P. Jervis, ed., *The Encyclopedia of Ceramics* (New York 1902), 36.

11 Edwin A. Barber, *Anglo-American Pottery* (Indianapolis 1899), 33.

12 Ellouise Baker Larsen, *American Historical Views on Staffordshire China* (Garden City, NY 1950), 31.

13 Elizabeth Collard, *Nineteenth-Century Pottery and Porcelain in Canada* (Montreal 1967), 204.

14 James Dixon, *Personal Narrative of a Tour Through a Part of the United States and Canada* (New York 1849), 110, 116–17.

15 *New York Observer* quoted in the *Niagara Mail*, 22 Dec. 1847.

16 Edward Allen Talbot, *Five Years' Residence in the Canadas* (London 1824), 1: 129.

17 Isabella Lucy Bird, *The Englishwoman in America* (1856; reprint, Toronto 1966), 234.

18 *Gazette* (Montreal), 25 July 1867.

19 M.M. Quaife, ed., *John Long's Voyages and Travels in the Years 1768–1788* (Chicago 1922), 5.

20 Benjamin Silliman, *A Tour to Quebec in the Autumn of 1819* (London 1822), 86.

21 Larsen, *American Historical Views*, 31.

22 Ross Robertson, ed., *The Diary of Mrs. John Graves Simcoe* (Toronto 1911), 75; Douglas S. Robertson, ed., *An Englishman in America 1785 Being the Diary of Joseph Hadfield* (Toronto 1933), 135–6.

23 [John Cosens Ogden], *A Tour Through Upper and Lower Canada* (Litchfield 1799), 31–3.

24 Robertson, ed., *An Englishman in America*, 123.

25 Silliman, *A Tour to Quebec*, 99.

26 Ibid. 102n.

27 Earle, *China Collecting in America*, 362. Larsen, *American Historical Views*, 21, lists only plates (dinner and soup).

4 POTTERS AND PADDLE-WHEELERS

1 James Dixon, *Personal Narrative of a Tour Through a Part of the United States and Canada* (New York 1849), 12.

2 B.K. Sandwell, *The Molson Family* (Montreal 1933), 39.

3 Canniff Haight, "Ontario Fifty Years Ago and Now," *Canadian Monthly and National Review*, May 1881, 453.

4 Sandwell, *The Molson Family*, 48.

5 Merrill Denison, *The Barley and the Stream* (Toronto 1955), 96.

6 See, for example, the advertisement in the *Montreal Transcript*, 12 Nov. 1836.

7 John M. Duncan quoted in Gerald M. Craig, ed., *Early Travellers in the Canadas* (Toronto 1955), 53.

8 *Kingston Chronicle*, 7 Jan. 1820.

9 James Strachan, *A Visit to the Province of Upper Canada in 1819* (Aberdeen 1820), 23–4.

10 His birth date is variously given. His obituary in the *Gazette* (16 July 1886) gives 1795, but census returns, for which he presumably supplied the information, would indicate a date closer to 1800. See the Montreal returns for 1861, for example.

11 Henry Allen Wedgwood quoted in John Thomas, ed., *People of the Potteries* (Bath 1970), 95.

12 *Canadian Courant*, 29 April 1820.

13 He advertised in *La Revue canadienne* (Montreal) on 5 May 1848 as a china merchant, but added: "N.B. M Bourne travaille toujours comme GRAVEUR au même lieu." In the 1861 census returns he listed himself as a china importer with a stock worth $16,000.

14 See for example their advertisement in the *Montreal Transcript*, 27 July 1839.

15 According to the *Canadian Courant* (Montreal), 25 July 1832, Bourne returned from England in the early summer of 1832.

16 He brought back with him a lithographic press. *Canadian Courant*, 25 July 1832.

17 Wolf Mankowitz and Reginald G. Haggar, *The Concise Encyclopedia of English Pottery and Porcelain* (London 1957), 21.

18 T.A. Lockett, *Davenport Pottery and Porcelain 1794–1887* (Newton Abbot 1972), 56.

19 Geoffrey Godden, *An Illustrated Encyclopaedia of British Pottery and Porcelain* (London 1966), 116 and pl. v.

20 *Missiskoui Standard* (Frelighsburg), 2 June 1835.

21 Elizabeth Collard, *Nineteenth-Century Pottery and Porcelain in Canada* (Montreal 1967), 244.

22 Lady Aylmer, "Recollections of Canada 1831," *Rapport de l'archiviste de la province de Québec pour 1934–1935* (Quebec n.d.), 305.

23 Elizabeth Collard, "An Exciting Discovery: A hitherto unrecorded view of Montreal," *Canadian Collector*, May–June 1981, 40–2.

24 I am indebted for this information to George Gibb.

25 *A Few Plain Directions for Persons Intending*

to *Proceed as Settlers to His Majesty's Province of Upper Canada* ... (London 1820), 41.

26 *A Cheering Voice from Upper Canada* (London 1834), 12.

27 Hon. Charles Grey (son of Lord Grey of the Reform Bill) who came to Canada in 1838. William Ormsby, ed., *Crisis in the Canadas: 1838–1839. The Grey Journals and Letters* (Toronto 1965), 17.

5 VIEWING THE CUNARDERS

1 Samuel Cunard quoted in Phyllis R. Blakeley, "Sir Samuel Cunard," *Dictionary of Canadian Biography* (Toronto 1976), IX: 179–80.

2 *Montreal Gazette*, 2 Oct. 1841.

3 Reginald Haggar and Elizabeth Adams, *Mason Porcelain and Ironstone 1796–1853* (London 1977), 76.

4 For an illustration of a plate with this design see Geoffrey Godden, *The Illustrated Guide to Mason's Patent Ironstone China* (London 1971), pl. 76. The mark on these Mason's plates is the usual printed mark with a crown and the words MASON'S PATENT IRONSTONE CHINA.

5 For typical advertisements for mulberry-coloured wares see the *Montreal Gazette*, 17 Oct. 1850 and 1 July 1851. Wares advertised in Canada in 1850 or 1851 were probably made towards the end of the 1840s.

6 Jackson's name appears on earthenware printed in a floral pattern that has also been recorded with the name of Samuel Alcorn, a Quebec City importer active in the 1830s and 1840s.

7 M.B. Buckley, *Diary of a Tour in America* (Dublin 1886), 4. The diary was not published until some years after the trip had been undertaken. Kate Buckley, sister of the diarist, prepared it for publication, issuing it privately.

8 Charles Dickens, *American Notes* (London 1842), I: 2–3.

9 I am indebted to John Munday, Keeper, Department of Weapons and Antiquities at the National Maritime Museum, London (England), for telling me of the album of lithographic sheets in the museum's possession.

10 Dickens, *American Notes*, I: 2, 4, 7.

11 James Dixon, *Personal Narrative of a Tour Through a Part of the United States and Canada* (New York 1849), 13.

12 Ibid. 18–19.

13 On the safety of the letters and the dependable delivery of the mails Cunard's reputation would stand or fall. Packet services, as Parry noted, were "established *solely* for the conveyance of letters." The conveyance of passengers was "merely an *incidental* advantage to the public, not directly intended by the system." Parry quoted in Ann Parry, *Parry of the Arctic* (London 1963), 195.

14 Llewellynn Jewitt, *The Ceramic Art of Great Britain* (London 1883), 456. Jewitt says James Edwards "commenced entirely on his own account" in 1842. Some modern books of reference give 1841 as the year the partnership was terminated, less than four months after the "Boston Mails" was registered by the firm of J. & T. Edwards (the registration is under the brothers' joint names at the Patent Office). See Geoffrey Godden, *Encyclopaedia of British Pottery and Porcelain Marks* (London 1964), 231.

15 Elizabeth Collard, *Nineteenth-Century Pottery and Porcelain in Canada* (Montreal 1967), 233.

16 The firm was officially James Edwards & Son by 1851 and exhibited under that business style at the Great Exhibition. See *Great Exhibition of the Works of Industry of all Nations, 1851. Official Descriptive and Illustrated Catalogue* (London 1851), II: 725. The catalogue listing is actually "J.

Edwards & Sons," but Jewitt speaks only of James' taking his son Richard into partnership, so that "Sons" is probably a misprint for "Son."

17 *Liverpool Times*, 29 April 1865, reprinted in the *Montreal Gazette*, 17 May 1865.

6 ARCTIC SCENERY

1 *Montreal Gazette*, 11 Jan. 1834.

2 From a letter of 1827 quoted in Robert Legget, *Rideau Waterway* (Toronto 1955), 194.

3 William Edward Parry, *Journal of a Voyage for the Discovery of a North-West Passage From the Atlantic to the Pacific; Performed in the Years 1819–20 in His Majesty's Ships Hecla and Griper* (London 1821), 125.

4 *Montreal Gazette*, 26 Oct. 1861.

5 See John Ross, *Appendix to the Narrative of a Second Voyage in Search of a North-West Passage and of a Residence in the Arctic Regions* (London 1835), lxxiv, lxxv, xcii. William Taylor Copeland, who was both a London alderman and a member of parliament, is erroneously listed here as "Thomas" Copeland.

6 Robert McClure, private journal, quoted in Noel Wright, *Quest for Franklin* (London 1959), 191–2.

7 Information supplied by Miss M.R. Clarke, a great-grandniece of Hannah Schneider.

8 For example, figures, sledges, and dogs on some of this earthenware have been taken from "The Ostiacks method of travelling in Winter," one of the illustrations in Thomas Bankes, *A Modern, Authentic and Complete System of Geography ...* (London n.d.). The illustrations were variously placed by the binders in this late eighteenth-century work.

7 BARTLETT'S CANADIAN SCENERY

1 William Beattie, *A Brief Memoir of William Henry Bartlett* (London 1855), in Alexan-

der M. Ross, *William Henry Bartlett: Artist, Author, Traveller* (Toronto 1973), 123.

2 "The Potteries," *Art Union*, May 1844, 107.

3 J.W. MacKail, *Studies of English Poets* (London 1926), 244.

4 Beattie, *William Henry Bartlett*, 101.

5 *Evening Express and Commercial Record* (Halifax), 21 Dec. 1866.

6 Elizabeth Collard, *Nineteenth-Century Pottery and Porcelain in Canada* (Montreal 1967), 211–16.

7 Beattie, *William Henry Bartlett*, 124.

8 *Montreal Gazette*, 30 Dec. 1861.

9 *Art Journal*, Jan. 1855, 24.

10 S.C. Hall, *Retrospect of a Long Life* (New York 1883), 421.

11 Van Wyck Brooks, *The World of Washington Irving* (New York 1944), 433.

12 Beattie, *William Henry Bartlett*, 136.

13 Ibid.

14 Ibid. 141.

15 Ibid. 123.

16 *Royal Gazette* (Fredericton), 21 Oct. 1840.

17 Beattie, *William Henry Bartlett*, 146.

18 Elizabeth Collard, "Nineteenth-Century Canadian Importers' Marks," *Material History Bulletin*, Museum of Man, History Division, Ottawa, no. 16 (1982), 24. After Thomas and Benjamin Godwin dissolved partnership each continued potting on his own.

19 I am indebted for the information on Enoch Wedgwood to Arnold Mountford, Director of Museums, City of Stoke-on-Trent, Staffordshire.

20 The plate, early Victorian in date, was handed down in the family of Dr Eugene Forsey. It is illustrated in Elizabeth Collard, "China for Children," *Canadian Collector*, Nov. 1982, 27. Children's plates of this type were made by many potters, but are very often unmarked.

21 Elizabeth Collard, *Nineteenth-Century Pottery*, 211.

22 The plate is now in the possession of Dr R.P. Harpur.

8 MORLEY'S BARTLETT VIEWS

1 Reginald G. Haggar, *The Masons of Lane Delph* (1952), 95.
2 Elizabeth Collard, *Nineteenth-Century Pottery and Porcelain in Canada* (Montreal 1967), 196.
3 Haggar, *The Masons of Lane Delph*, 83.
4 The partnership in this case was William Ridgway, Son & Co.
5 *Royal Gazette* (Fredericton), 21 Oct. 1840.
6 Haggar, *The Masons of Lane Delph*, 95.
7 Ibid.
8 Llewellynn Jewitt, *The Ceramic Art of Great Britain* (London 1878), II: 316.
9 Haggar, *The Masons of Lane Delph*, 53.
10 M. Digby Wyatt, *On the Influence Exercised on Ceramic Manufactures by the Late Mr. Herbert Minton* (London 1858), 27 (a paper read before the Society of Arts on 26 May 1858 and later privately published by Wyatt).
11 Found as part of Spode's Caramanian series.
12 Jewitt, *The Ceramic Art of Great Britain*, 316; Haggar, *The Masons of Lane Delph*, 61. See also Reginald Haggar and Elizabeth Adams, *Mason Porcelain and Ironstone 1796–1853* (London 1977), 99. It should be noted that Mason's shapes were also copied by others with less right to them than Morley.
13 The collections of the National Museum of Man include a plate with the name of the Philadelphia importers Tyndale & Mitchell. This is the importer's mark most frequently encountered, but others have been recorded. The "Lake" pattern was not, of course, made expressly for any one importer anywhere. The presence of an importer's mark on a piece merely indicates that that particular importer was distributing the pattern in his city or area.
14 Personal communication from Miss Clare Harrington (a granddaughter of Sir William and Lady Dawson).
15 Personal communication from J.S. Goddard.
16 Some earthenware potters impressed the word IVORY on their tablewares; others advertised their new "Ivory Body." Porcelain makers, too, such as Worcester, had an "ivory" ware. It was all part of the Victorian interest in ivory as a material with many decorative uses. So great was the interest and so widespread the use of ivory itself that Canadian newspapers used to report on the English sales of the raw material (see, for example, the Montreal *Daily Witness*, 29 Nov. 1882).
17 Personal communication from J.S. Goddard.
18 Jewitt, *The Ceramic Art of Great Britain*, 316.

9 MAPLE LEAVES AND BEAVERS

1 Hubert LaRue, *Le Bulletin des recherches historiques* IV, no. 1 (Jan. 1898): 119.
2 Gédéon de Catalogne, letter from Quebec, 7 Sept. 1712, *Le Bulletin des recherches historiques* XXI, no. 9 (Sept. 1915): 259.
3 LaRue, *Le Bulletin des recherches historiques*, 119.
4 Ibid. 119–20.
5 C.W. Dilke, *Greater Britain: A Record of Travel in English-Speaking Countries During 1866 and 1867* (London 1868), I: 69.
6 Brian Young, *George-Etienne Cartier: Montreal Bourgeois* (Kingston and Montreal 1981), 92.
7 Massicotte made a note to this effect when he presented examples of the ware to the Château de Ramezay in Montreal. The full note, in Massicotte's handwriting, was shown to the author some thirty years ago by Louis Carrier, then curator of the château.
8 Samuel Thompson, "Reminiscences of a Canadian Pioneer," *Canadian Monthly* VII (July–Dec. 1881): 631.

9 Douglas Brymner, the first Dominion archivist, believed this to be the case. See Horace T. Martin, *Castorologia or the History and Traditions of the Canadian Beaver* (Montreal and London 1892), 198.

10 J.W. Dawson, *Duties of Educated Young Men in British America* (Montreal [1863]), 2.

11 Ibid.

12 *Daily Witness* (Montreal), 31 Aug. 1881.

13 Invoice in the possession of Ted Boulerice, formerly of Parks Canada, Ottawa.

14 Examples of this ware are to be seen in the Royal Canadian Mounted Police Museum, Regina.

15 Eaton's catalogues describe these articles as "butter pads." See, for example, *Catalogue No. 28: Fall and Winter 1894–95*, 96.

16 Information from J. Bailey, Managing Director, Furnivals (1913) Ltd.

17 In 1939 what remained of this service was in the possession of a member of the Pope family and was shown to the author at that time.

10 CANADIAN SPORTS

1 W. George Beers, *Over the Snow* (Montreal 1883), 8.

2 William Howard Russell, *Canada: Its Defences, Condition, and Resources* (London 1865), 84.

3 Sarah Thompson, letter written from Belleville, Canada West, 5 Nov. 1857. Unpublished letter in author's possession.

4 W. George Beers, "Canada in Winter," *British American Magazine*, Nov. 1863, 170.

5 *Daily Witness* (Montreal), 24 Nov. 1881; 6 Dec. 1881.

6 Elizabeth Collard, "Canada's Victorian Christmas Cards," *Canadian Collector*, Nov.–Dec. 1974, 37.

7 *Gazette* (Montreal), 18 Dec. 1882.

8 *Daily Witness*, 5 Dec. 1888.

9 Llewellynn Jewitt, *The Ceramic Art of Great Britain* (London 1878), I: 521.

10 According to Geoffrey Godden, it closed in 1899, with "Ltd." becoming part of the mark in 1897. Geoffrey Godden, *Encyclopaedia of British Pottery and Porcelain Marks* (London 1964), 414. A date just slightly earlier for the closing has been given by some other writers.

11 Elizabeth Collard, *Nineteenth-Century Pottery and Porcelain in Canada* (Montreal 1967), 225.

12 H. Symons, *Fences* (Toronto 1958), xiii.

13 See, for example, the complaint of the Montreal Hunt Club in the *Gazette*, 23 Feb. 1883.

14 The pattern, which had a long life, was originally introduced at the Bo'ness Pottery by James Jamieson & Co. When Marshall took over the business he continued it.

15 It appears in invoices of crockery Laflamme purchased from a Montreal importing and wholesale house with Scottish connections (for example, in an invoice dated 29 May 1882, in the possession of Ted Boulerice).

16 *Saturday Night* (Toronto), 18 Feb. 1899.

17 *Gazette* (Montreal), 7 Oct. 1867. "Seconds," edged, and sponged wares (all lower priced goods) were in this trade sale.

18 Beers, *Over the Snow*, 30, 36.

11 PHOTOGRAPHS AND THE POTTER

1 Mary FitzGibbon, *A Trip to Manitoba* (London 1880), 89.

2 Advertisements make this clear. See, for example, advertisements for photograph albums in: *Morning Chronicle* (Quebec), 7 June 1862; *Protestant and Evangelical Witness* (Charlottetown), 6 Dec. 1862; *Evening Express and Commercial Record* (Halifax), 4 Jan. 1864.

3 Charles Gibbon, "All a Green Willow,"

Canadian Monthly and National Review, July 1879, 37–8.

4 A.H. Malan, "On Illuminating an Album," *Cassell's Family Magazine*, Sept. 1880, 597.

5 It is so listed in *Lovell's ... Business Directory of the Province of Quebec, 1910–11*.

6 J. Arnold Fleming, *Scottish Pottery* (Glasgow 1923), 103, 111.

7 Ibid. 109.

8 *Canadian Illustrated News* (Montreal), 21 June 1879.

9 Marius Barbeau, "Canadian Pottery," *Antiques*, June 1941, 297.

10 Marius Barbeau, *Maîtres Artisans de cheznous* (Montreal 1942), 127. Barbeau was born in 1883.

11 J. Arnold Fleming, *Scottish Pottery*, 115. As the Britannia Pottery Co. Ltd, the business continued into the 1930s.

12 See, for example, the *Daily Witness* (Montreal), 4 July 1885.

13 Elizabeth Collard, "Tracing the Source of the 'Thomas Views,'" *Canadian Collector*, Sept.–Oct. 1976, 23–5.

14 At the Ministry of Agriculture, Ottawa (at that time responsible for Canadian copyright).

15 T.L. Boulanger and E. Marcotte, eds., *The Quebec Indicator* (Quebec 1889), 86.

16 Personal communication from Ralph Greenhill.

17 He advertised them in Boulanger and Marcotte, *The Quebec Indicator*, as "Holiwell's Album Views of Quebec."

18 The title page is reproduced in Ralph Greenhill, *Early Photography in Canada* (Toronto 1965), 47.

19 *Morning Chronicle* (Quebec), 20 Dec. 1864.

12 MISCELLANEOUS CANADIAN VIEWS

1 [James Pattison Cockburn], *Quebec and Its Environs; Being a Picturesque Guide to the Stranger* (Quebec 1831), 3–4.

2 Alfred Hawkins, *Picture of Quebec* (Quebec 1834), 6–7.

3 Ellouise Baker Larsen, *American Historical Views on Staffordshire China* (Garden City, NY 1950), 206, 208, 210.

4 Richard H. Wood and Virginia A. Wood, *Historical China Cup Plates* (Baltimore, n.d.), item no. 20.

5 Larsen, *American Historical Views*, 34, 63.

6 The firm's working dates are variously given. Robert Nicholls, writing the history of the Adams family, says the Clews brothers rented their pot works from William Adams in 1817. Robert Nicholls, *Ten Generations of a Potting Family* (London, n.d.), 84. See also Wolf Mankowitz and Reginald G. Haggar, *The Concise Encyclopedia of English Pottery and Porcelain* (London 1957), 55.

7 Larsen, *American Historical Views*, 207.

8 What remained of the service descended to his great-granddaughter, Miss Isabelle Galer Cheesman.

9 For a discussion of Clementson's Canadian connections see Elizabeth Collard, *Nineteenth-Century Pottery and Porcelain in Canada* (Montreal 1967), 80–4; also Collard, "Clementson Wares: An Opportunity for the China Collector," *Canadian Antiques & Art Review*, Oct. 1980, 26–9.

10 All the favourite mid-century components were present: a vista with water, a sailing boat, rustic buildings of the European type, a graceful tree, and figures.

11 The same border and same name, "Toronto," were also used with an imaginary scene (flowers and ruins) replacing the geometrical centre design.

12 M.J. Loftie, *The Dining Room* (London 1878), 109.

13 Llewellynn Jewitt, *The Ceramic Art of Great Britain* (London 1883), 449.

14 1884 is the date usually given for the beginning of Wallis Gimson & Co., but records at the City Museum and Art Gallery, in Stoke-on-Trent, Staffordshire,

show that the date was actually 1883. Information from Arnold Mountford, director of the City Museum and Art Gallery.

15 Information from Mrs William Tetley.

16 Louisa Stacey, July 1851, to E.G. Stacey; cited in Jane Vansittart, ed., *Lifelines: The Stacey Letters, 1836–1858* (London 1976), 122.

17 William Dawson, *Fifty Years of Work in Canada* (London 1901), 181.

18 *Toronto Daily Mail*, 23 Dec. 1886. The Parian statuettes of the Princess Louise and the Marquis of Lorne were also available in earthenware in the type of figure known today as "Staffordshire figures."

INDEX

See also Glossary